# read me first

## Lisa Stephenson

First published in 2018 by Major Street Publishing Pty Ltd.
Reprinted in 2022.
PO Box 106, Highett, Vic. 3190 E: info@majorstreet.com.au
W: majorstreet.com.au M: +61 421 707 983

**Ordering information**

**Quantity sales.** Special discounts are available on quantity purchases by corporations, associations and others. For details, contact Lesley Williams using the contact details above.

**Individual sales.** Major Street publications are available through most bookstores. They can also be ordered directly from Major Street's online bookstore at www.majorstreet.com.au/shop.

The moral rights of the author have been asserted.

A catalogue record for this book is available from the National Library of Australia

NATIONAL LIBRARY OF AUSTRALIA

ISBN: 978-0-6482387-6-8

Internal design by Production Works
Cover design by Simone Geary
Photograph: Kirsty Duchet; Stylist: Candice Lewin; Hair and make-up: Carlie Christie
Printed in Australia by IVE Group, an Accredited ISO AS/NZS 14001:2004 Environmental Management System Printer

10 9 8 7 6 5 4 3 2

Disclaimer: The material in this publication is in the nature of general comment only, and neither purports nor intends to be advice. Readers should not act on the basis of any matter in this publication without considering (and if appropriate taking) professional advice with due regard to their own particular circumstances. The author and publisher expressly disclaim all and any liability to any person, whether a purchaser of this publication or not, in respect of anything and the consequences of anything done or omitted to be done by any such person in reliance, whether whole or partial, upon the whole or any part of the contents of this publication.

## Praise for Lisa Stephenson and *Read Me First*

Over a career, you run across maybe a handful of truly exceptional practitioners, individuals whose abilities deliver something unique in their field. Lisa is one of those individuals. Her accessible and supportive style underpin what is a deeply challenging approach to personal and professional growth... An approach that sets the standard when it comes to building strong and independent leaders.

**David Hornery | Co-CEO | Judo Capital**

Reading this book took me on the journey again. It brought back all the memories and the feelings of uncertainty that I had when transitioning out from playing AFL football. But, just like in my many catch-ups with Lisa, the belief, clarity and self-confidence came back and the future wasn't daunting anymore. The process you go on, and the questions that Lisa holds you accountable to, can be raw and confronting, although they are absolutely required and completely necessary to keep moving forward. Lisa's ability to understand what is important to you and what makes you happy is unique, as is her sense of humour that shines through in this book. Lisa asks the right questions so that you can define what success really means. This book will challenge everything you think you know about yourself. Take the risk, own the process and do the work on yourself. That's what Lisa told me to do and so I did. Enjoy the read and the rewards!

**Nick Dal Santo | Sports Broadcaster, Speaker and Former AFL Player**

I met Lisa Stephenson at an extremely challenging time in my life. My regular coaching sessions with Lisa were essential in initially assessing my personal and professional situation and taking the steps towards being and achieving who and what I wanted to be. Having Lisa in my corner as my coach was a crucial part of getting to where I am today. Her coaching instincts are invaluable when it comes to mindset, and she has a way of connecting that makes you trust upfront. A five-minute phone call or two-hour sit-down with Lisa provided me with both strategic coaching sessions and in-situ problem-solving. These different styles were crucial and a large part of her dynamic, caring and result-driven process. Thank you Lisa.

**James Hird | Former AFL Player and Coach**

I am one of those people who has been lucky enough to meet Lisa through the amazing work she does and I now call her a friend. Over the last few years I have seen the impact of both Lisa's individual coaching and group coaching sessions. I've also seen her in action presenting to large groups as a keynote speaker. In each interaction, her warmth, humour and genuine commitment to support each and every person to be the very best they can be shines through. Reading this book is just like sitting with her and receiving your own personal coaching session. *Read Me First* asks the same insightful questions, has the same outrageous sense of fun and the very real sense of being lovingly supported through your discomfort. Her own personal story gives great insight into what it takes to create success and happiness on a personal and professional level. If you can't get in a room with her, this book is the next best thing. It really is just so perfectly Lisa, hugs and all. I am a fan and know lots of others who are too.

**Natalie Thomas | Shoe Fanatic and Raging LS Fan**

I love Lisa Stephenson's book! She brings her life stories, her experience as a coach and her humour all together in this book. She knows how to encourage and help us to be the best we can be. Lisa knows how to get you past the challenges that happen in life and come out victorious. Lisa has also been a keynote speaker at four of the recent Financial Executive Women (FEW) conferences held across Australia and was continually rated as excellent. She is intuitive and has a way of connecting that really brings the room together. Her ability to tell a story that people can relate to, use her coaching abilities to identify solutions and ask thought-provoking questions is a real strength. I recommend *Read Me First* to anyone who wants guidance on how to start their next journey, to simply look at things differently and ask the right questions about who they are and where they want to go. A great, easy read that at a minimum will leave you reflective, thoughtful and wanting to consciously create your next chapter.

**Judith Beck | CEO and Founder | Financial Executive Women (FEW)**

Lisa Stephenson is undoubtedly the Queen of Personal Branding. Her capacity to distil a lifetime of personal experience and two decades of coaching wisdom (and a huge dose of in-your-face humour) has enabled her to tap into the holy grail of human development. When she asks 'Who Am I ...?' Lisa gently grabs your hand and guides you through the most enlightening, confronting and sometimes scary labyrinth towards the ultimate version of yourself. Her expertise in getting you to ask yourself the right questions at the right time is unparalleled, and this is her (not so) secret weapon. In this book, Lisa generously shares with you her usually behind-closed-doors methodology and lifts the curtain on a range of insights and practical tools you can use today. My advice to you, dear reader, is to take this book and devour it! Listen to her stories, hear her advice and, most importantly, act on her suggestions. This. Stuff. Works.

**Melanie Schilling | Psychologist and Massive LS Fan**

I have had the privilege of experiencing the impact of Lisa's work over the past seven years – actually it never looks like work because for Lisa it is a labour of love. Lisa has the unique ability to connect to people by asking them questions and provoking them to think about things they may have never considered before. Her approach is both instinctive and intuitive and right for the person and the time – she knows when to push to get the best out of the individual. I have personally experienced the 'encouragement' and the results. It has truly defined me as a leader.

This book beautifully captures the experience she creates for her clients. It is warm, thought-provoking and encourages the reader to be responsible for their own success. As someone who has personally experienced the transformation that is possible when you work with Lisa, it is with respect that I invite you to enjoy *Read Me First*. I do so knowing what is possible if you step into the process with courage and an open heart.

As a leader in corporate Australia who has invested heavily in leaders 'doing deep work on themselves', I often ponder what the world would be like if all leaders made this investment. I truly believe that there is strength in vulnerability, and Lisa's approach will invite you to consider the impact you can have by being your authentic self. Enjoy!

**Cindy Batchelor | EGM | NAB Business**

It is a gift to be able to explore, explain and navigate the potentially deep, complicated and laborious subject matter that is 'self-management' on a physical, mental, emotional, behavioural and sociological level without confusing (or boring) the crap out of the reader. I call it 'Lisa-fication' (noun) or to 'Lisa-fy' (verb). Call it whatever you like but Lisa Stephenson has produced a book that not only shares great insights, advice and strategies for life but is also a body of work that's funny, relatable, relevant and powerful.

**Craig Harper | Author, Speaker and Media Presenter**

Lisa Stephenson has that unique blend of warmth, empathy, wit and smarts that make her an invaluable leader, coach and teacher. Her life's work is to share her wisdom and help others to live and lead better, and in this book she nails the brief.

**Mia Freedman | Co-founder and Content Director | Mamamia Women's Network**

I loved reading this! A straight-up, real and raw manual to living life the way we're meant to – truly awake to our purpose.

**Andrea Clarke | Founder | CareerCEO**

The first time you meet Lisa is like meeting a very old friend. Her warmth and care create a safe and nurturing environment. Lisa uses that safe place to really challenge you, to ask questions that provoke and help you to dig into your values and what really matters. The work is hard, really hard, yet the rewards are life-changing. Whether you are an established entrepreneur, inspiring leader, struggling parent or just ready for a career change, *Read Me First* will both structure your thinking and honour your future plans.

What I admire about Lisa is her resilience, her fundamental belief and investment in the power of relationships and her unwavering commitment to her family. Lisa is someone you want in your circle. The power of her positivity and the integrity with which she lives her life is inspiring. I will be forever grateful to have met Lisa and I look forward to watching this next chapter in her life. *Read Me First* gives everyone access to her coaching questions, insightful thoughts and the strategies I've seen her use with hundreds of people.

**Melanie Hilton | GM Operational Risk and Financial Crime | Westpac Group**

Lisa Stephenson has been my success coach for the past three years. In that time, I have engaged her to work with my leadership teams in both Asia and America. She has a way of working that is both confronting and supportive, she brings huge energy and passion to every meeting, event and coaching session and keeps it very real. My work with Lisa Stephenson has brought to life the leader I want to be in my career and at home.

Lisa is strategic, thoughtful and skilled in her approach. She doesn't let you get away with anything. She sees you for who you really are and who you have the potential to be. She puts her heart and trust in every single person she meets. *Read Me First* is absolutely a reflection of the journey she has taken me on. I am a better husband, dad, friend and leader because of Lisa.

**Andrew O'Brien | Executive Vice-President Customer and Sales North America | Treasury Wine Estates**

Lisa is a brilliant combination of integrity, wisdom, authenticity and humour. In *Read Me First*, she fuses together decades of coaching and mentoring experience with gritty real-life substance. Lisa is an unstoppable force in supporting people to transform their lives.

**Jacqui Lewis | Founder | The Broad Place**

*To Mabel, William and James*
*because we are the Stephenson tribe!*

*This was not my plan for us, but look at us go!*
*Being your mum is the most amazing adventure.*
*I love you more than dolphins and Nutella.*

*And because I am a rule breaker, I am going*
*to have another dedication:*

*To the readers of this book,*
*I like the future version of you a lot!*

# Caution

This book alone will not change your life, but **you** can.

Whether you succeed or fail in life is up to you.

So take responsibility for you, and be ready to take action. (Just don't make big decisions after wine consumption.)

This book is about coaching yourself to success, whatever success means for you.

Herein you will find:

- ► Thought-provokers for redesigning your life
- ► Coaching questions that challenge your thinking
- ► Practical strategies for creating a successful life
- ► Life 'must-haves' for an emotionally healthy you
- ► Ways to build momentum for your next chapter
- ► Tips on how to communicate your story, if that matters to you.

# Contents

## Part III: Strategies for a successful life 121

## Part IV: 10 life must-haves 155

## Part V: Your story's next chapter 173

## About the author
# The nice bit

I am a global speaker with over 20 years' experience in senior management roles, entrepreneurship, success coaching and event facilitation. I have been called lots of other things too; high performance coach, life coach and executive coach. You can call me anything you like!

I am the founding director of the internationally regarded thecoachplace.com and creator of the 'I am...' statement and 'Leadership Point of View' statement. I have worked around the globe with my team of highly experienced facilitators and coaches. I love what I do.

I have worked as a high performance coach with an array of global corporate organisations, CEOs, celebrities, elite athletes, media personalities, senior leaders and other talented individuals. I am often referred to as 'Lisa the trusted adviser'.

But who am I really?

Well, I'm an Aperol Spritz lover. I am imperfect. I live with authenticity and am the best secret-keeper around! I get grumpy when I'm tired and am known for eating cereal for dinner. I laugh at inappropriate things. (I don't swear often but laugh out loud when others do.) I dislike gyms, but I go because I know it's good for me.

I suspect the professional coaching community has raised their collective eyebrows at me on occasion. I rebel against rules and protocols and negativity and limits. I think it's really important to have regrets. I've made plenty of mistakes and continue to work on me.

I'm a committed advocate for people to step up and go after what they want in life. I am passionate about many things, including emotionally intelligent living and finding a way to thrive in a time-poor, complex and challenging world.

A quick look at Instagram will show you my work around Australia and my frequent visits to America, the UK and Asia as I challenge people's thinking and share my thoughts on why we behave the way we do. I am one of those people who finds brains fascinating, and people-watching at the airport is my version of fun.

I appreciate that I am valued for provoking people; I am known for going hard on the issues but not the person, asking the questions that hurt, dismissing the excuses that hold people back and holding people (teams, organisations and groups) accountable for their own successes and failures.

I was born to coach; being intuitive and empathetic is my super power. I speak from the heart of who we (each) are, what we (really) want for ourselves, and what we have to do (the work) to get from where we are to where we would rather be. Whether working with a crowd of a thousand or an individual, I am walking my talk and being my best self (most of the time) and building trust and relationships at the speed of light! I am about transformational moments and BIG results.

## In a nutshell

- ► I call the Mornington Peninsula (Australia) home, and have three awesome children, a naughty dog, some half-dead fish, a possum in the roof and a house recently renovated (what was I thinking?).

- ► I've done 20 years of coaching, consulting, leadership and facilitating; I created my consulting business nine years ago when I quite suddenly became a single mum.

- ► My personal experiences of divorce, grief, single parenthood and building a global business mean this book has been written with compassion, insight and a whole load of interesting life experience.

- ► I've been on more flights than I can count and fantasise about eight hours sleep a night. I love to travel and love the beach.

- ► I have a wicked sense of humour and maybe laugh too loud and too often – especially at my own jokes.

- ► I'm a bit obsessed with Instagram, all things Italian, good wine and getting things done yesterday!

- ► I'm looking for a man to share my life with. If that may be you, get in touch! (I have many dating stories, but those are for another book.)

- ► I am lots of fun! Although I should probably check that with my children.

My approach to business is entrepreneurial. In addition to my global consulting business, I operate a private coaching practice, am a regular on the speaking circuit and mentor many high-profile leaders. To satisfy my need for travel and sparkle, I am also on the advisory board to the stunning fashion label Aneka Manners (www.anekamanners.com.au).

This book comes from all that I currently know, all that I've studied, observed, heard and discussed. I'm a professional, qualified, highly regarded and experienced coach. I've asked thousands of the difficult questions, had thousands of the difficult conversations, and I listen ever so well. That's what coaches do. This book is about what I've seen successful people do and why. This is about what I know works. Tried and tested!

But, mostly, this book is about you and your next chapter.

# The good, the bad and the ugly

I wrote this book because nine years ago every certainty I knew about life collapsed. That sounds so dramatic now, but that was absolutely my truth then. I had to create a career that would provide financially for my three little people and myself, and work out what my new version of success would be. My beautiful life, the previous chapter in my story, had abruptly come to a very definite end. The old story of me was a simple one and I had loved it. I wanted a great marriage to my best friend, to be a mostly at home mum, while coaching some clients along the way because I had always loved to work.

Yet here I was feeling ill-equipped to be a single full-time working mum and overwhelmed by how much there was to do. I was that woman! The one who had the rather traditional role of homemaker and mum, and part-time hours in the office to keep my hand in. My children were in a highly regarded private school and life was what I wanted it to be. He paid all the bills, managed our finances and did all the things a typical loving dad and husband would do. I had to find a way to now be the mum and the dad.

The easy option would have been to go and get a job. But if I was going to build an amazing life, I needed to make amazing choices. Simmering beneath the surface of uncertainty was a voice that I now know was the inner entrepreneur. I was quietly determined to draw on everything I had ever learned, read and experienced. This is the book I wish I had been able to pick up off the bookshelf. This is the book that captures the strategies I implemented and now want to share with you.

Let me start by saying I have some perspective. I am one of many when it comes to divorce, miscarriage, financial loss and emotional bankruptcy. There are many partners in the world who feel the impact of mental health issues, and there are people who have beaten challenges far greater than mine. My point is that we all have a story with lessons to learn and challenges to cope with. Bad things really do happen to good people. But it's what we do in the middle of a crisis that counts.

## There's nothing to see here!

My childhood story is a lovely one. My memories are full of laughter, family and bike-riding adventures. I grew up by the beach in Mooloolaba, Queensland, Australia. My parents were, and still are, married. Bless them! They love me more than life itself. I liked my school. I had friends. My brother was annoying and joyful. There wasn't a no-hat-no-play policy for children back then, so I had a great tan. I dreamed of working in a shoe shop with my best friend, Jacqui, and having a milkshake every day on our lunch break. We had a pool at home, which is heaven for kids. We went to a different beach for school holidays; Noosa and the Gold Coast were common fun destinations. My mum made me eat healthy food most of the time. My first kiss was with a cute boy named Adam.

My childhood wasn't perfect and it wasn't privileged but it was pretty close to that. We moved interstate when I was 13 and I hated leaving my friends. My new school would make me cry.

It was here that I had my head pushed down the toilet, and I had my first lessons in resilience. Then we moved again, this time to Melbourne and life was better.

I loved Melbourne on arrival and still love it now. For the most part, mine was a happy childhood and I was surrounded by love and family. My most traumatic loss was when someone stole my bike. I had everything I needed to set me up as a happy and healthy adult.

## Adulthood

At the age of 17 I went off to university. I had never had a 'real' boyfriend. I was innocent, terrified and beyond excited at the thought of living on my own and growing my independence in a super-cool regional town by the beach called Warrnambool, nearly four hours' drive away from home. Freedom! I met my future husband the day after I moved into my bedsit unit. I was engaged to him at 19 and married at 21. I finished my degree, started my career, did more study. We moved to London in 1999 to explore Europe and expand our careers. I was happily pregnant at 24 and a mum at 25. Life was great. I was married to my best friend; the only man I had ever loved.

We returned to Melbourne and I was taking my first baby steps into entrepreneurship in a coaching business with a friend and her husband. Four years later, there was another beautiful baby and, because he was so divine, two years after that a little girl was born. I had a home, a husband, a nice car and a safari to Africa to look forward to. I had the life I had always wanted. I appreciated how blessed I was.

## This was not my plan

It had never crossed my mind that one day I would be a single mum – ever. But in 2009 that is exactly what happened. The courts granted me full custody of my children; I reverted to my maiden name and so did my children. We moved house five times in seven years. The children moved schools three times in two years. I found myself so deep in grief that I forgot to eat and avoided sleep at all costs. How had this happened? It was as if aliens had come and stolen my husband. He was literally gone. There would be long periods of not knowing where he was or if he was even alive.

I cried secretly and smiled publicly. It became abundantly clear that my soon to be ex-husband would not take responsibility for our three little people in any way. He was knee-deep in depression. I call it that but neither of us, to this day, is really sure what label to give it. Essentially, he just decided that he no longer wanted to be a husband or father – full stop. Keeping us safe – emotionally, financially and physically – would become a full-time job for me. (Yes, I have his permission to share this with you, and actually he thought I was being too kind!)

In the following years, there would be so many tears and ongoing challenges to manage with the father of my children who no longer wanted to be a father. The suicide calls from him in the middle of the night would leave me sitting in the bottom of the shower, wondering how I would find the energy to keep him alive, while supporting my children and growing a business. I remember standing in court finalising our divorce and feeling like it was the saddest thing I had ever felt – the finality that it was over. This was a story I didn't know how to tell my children. Baked beans on toast for dinner was sometimes all I could manage. Each and every day started with the same questions: What will happen today? How can I make sure everyone is OK? How am I going to pay the rent? Will it ever not feel like this?

This chapter in my life tested me and I experienced all kinds of discrimination. Not the horrendous, dramatic kind that legitimately floods our TV screens, but the kind where banks would not loan to a self-employed, single mother because self-employed is the same as unemployed. Real estate agents would not rent a single mum of three a home without some cash being slipped into their hand. Life insurance is more expensive for single women with children because you are considered to be high risk due to the increased likelihood of mental health issues. Throughout this book, you will see I was so incredibly fortunate to also meet people who both trusted and supported me.

There are so many labels we wear in life. 'Divorcee' was not a label I had ever wanted to wear. Over and over I muttered to myself, 'This was not my plan'. I was not prepared. There was no money left. My best friend was gone. And then the next chapter began.

## Curiosity saved me

I remember sitting at my kitchen bench and deciding that I would be curious whenever my head and heart could manage it. I would imagine, dream, work, learn and wonder. I would ask questions and trust I could find the answers. In fact, I registered my business as Curious Consulting and started to read everything I could on curiosity. I would discover how habitual we are as adults. I would understand why change is so hard.

I would get why resilience matters more than most things. I would value great questions. I would learn to challenge my own beliefs and values. I would be curious about my potential and the future of my children.

Being curious offers a different lens to fear, concern and anger. I would go on to make lots of mistakes but also achieve more than I ever knew I was capable of. This chapter would be the making of me.

## Now

I am learning to date. (Don't even get me started!) My children are doing well. In fact, they are exceptional individuals. I have a global consulting business. I have taken my personal experiences and created programs, learning experientials and coaching sessions that support people in finding their version of success. The little girl who wanted to work in a shoe shop is a distant memory. But the woman who wanted a home that feels like a sanctuary, and children who trust they are loved, is here.

I so often hear stories of people who find out that they are stronger and smarter than they knew as a result of a significant and life-changing event. This book is about finding out who you can be without the drama and trauma.

This is a big statement I know, but we are all capable of more than we know. This is not about how smart you are, the resources you have access to or the talents you have; this is about doing the work that's required to live the life you want.

It has been my privilege to write this book for you. They say we all have a book in us (I'm not sure who 'they' are). May yours be an awesome story. Let's do it.

# My promise to you

This book will challenge your thinking and then provide a structured way to reflect and take action. You'll find quotes to inspire you and questions to ask yourself. This is a friendly reminder that you really will never get today, or tomorrow, again. I know that if you do the work on you, you will grow, you will change, and you will succeed. When you change, so does the world around you.

That is my promise.

Lisa xx

**No one is coming to
fix anything for you.
It really is all up to you."**

# How to use this book

- Please laugh at my jokes (because I think I'm funny and because laughter is medicinal and motivational).

- Remember our conversation is confidential (I won't tell anyone).

- Be honest with yourself (but kind to yourself).

- Do your own excuse-busting (and skip the blame game).

- WRITE, WRITE and WRITE! (I promise, it does make a difference.)

- Consider the consequences of doing nothing.

- Be prepared to get uncomfortable; this is where the real learning and change and success happens.

- While the thought-provokers in part II of the book are in deliberate order, you can open this book at any page and work on whatever feels right.

- Do not tell anyone you are reading a 'self-help' book because I don't like that term!

- Start today! There is no better time. Tomorrow (or Monday) may be too late. Take the first step now.

- I intend for this book to create a beautiful, soul-searching experience, but also be a highly practical working tool. So please write, scribble, highlight, rip stuff out, paste stuff in, carry it around, spill stuff on it... use it!

# Read this first...

Have you ever heard someone say, 'If only life came with a set of instructions'? I have – hundreds of times. Almost every client who walks through my door has uttered this at some point. *Read Me First* is the book I wish I could have given them.

In the middle of the madness and mayhem, the peaks and troughs, the lessons and laughter, the triumphs and tragedy, is the beautiful and complex YOU. The writer of your story. The CEO of your life.

Life is awesome, then it's hard, then it's awesome again. It's extraordinary, sometimes boring and occasionally heartbreaking. We start new projects, change direction and bring an end to things we thought might last forever. We rebuild and do it all over again. We are designed and destined to feel, love, win, lose and sometimes mess up – that's our 'humanness', our strength and our weakness. We go through it and we grow, and we keep growing and going.

Imagine what could happen if you:

- developed greater self-awareness – a key competency to increase your emotional intelligence. (Simply, what if you had a clear vision of what's not working for you?)

- worked on yourself so that you really 'knew' you, and what your thinking, behaviour, life goals and ways of being are about. (OMG, just imagine.)

- explored the 'story' of who you have been and who you want to be. (And you could communicate it to people in a way that's inspiring rather than unsure, unstructured or boring.)

- developed a broader, deeper, enhanced vision of yourself and of what success actually means to you. (That is, you understood where you wanted to go in life, instead of just sleepwalking through it, always falling back on your 'default' responses and behaviours.)

- became so curious about the potential of you that reading this book raised possibilities about your future you'd never considered before. (Exciting! Keep reading.)

- were more able to leverage your strengths, past experiences and best attributes. (Success has a lot more to do with what you're good at than what you're terrible at, yet strangely we often focus on the latter.)

- paid proper attention to what's already working in your life and what's not. Imagine if you took time to listen to those voices in your head, the ones that are calling (or screaming) out for something to be different. (Most of us do not need medication for these voices!)

- stepped out of the old place, the waiting place, the procrastinating place, the comfortable place, and started honouring and working for the best/happier/more successful future version of you.

**I'd like you to regard this book as essential reading *before* you set out on the next chapter of your life.**

In this book, I will bring the strategies, thoughts and questions, and YOU need to bring the talent, passion, courage, potential, resilience, attitude and humility. It's all connected: your story, your purpose, your fears, your journey. Where you have been and where you want to go are linked. This book is about acknowledging what you really want in your next chapter, making the best decisions you can, creating a great plan and taking decisive action.

**tip**

Before you get started, make sure you muster a little patience. When you are doing the work and creating the change, it can take a while to realise you've made the right choices. There are no quick fixes, but there is a new adventure waiting. There will be setbacks and some quick wins, so just keep going. I am yet to meet anyone who is really an overnight success.

Get your big boy/girl pants on, because things are about to get interesting!

# Part I
## The story of you – now

*To have a better life we must keep
choosing how we are living.*

**Albert Einstein**

G osh, Einstein was clever! But guess what? You are
too! Why? Because you've picked up this book and
are going to do more than read it; you're going
to take action. You recognise that knowing isn't
doing, don't you?

You've decided that you want to take action to change
something in your life. Great. Then it's time to pay attention
and it's time to be responsible for you. I promise you will never
regret taking time to work on you.

Think of this book as a personal coaching session, for
within these pages you'll find all the 'hot topics' that I've
repeatedly expounded as a success coach for over two decades.

*If you are totally happy with every aspect of who you are and
what you do, congratulations; you can put this back on the shelf. Be
off with you!*

If you're ready to write the next chapter in the book of you,
let's go.

# Chapter 1
# Where are you now?

You are a unique, complex, ever-evolving human with your own journey, your own story, your own next chapter. To know, and more consciously plan for, where you want to go you need first to get clarity around where you've been and where you are 'at' now. I promise, this is a necessary step. So, please, be patient and do this bit first.

A great way to explore your current state of being, and to raise your self-awareness, is to make yourself write down a description or a statement about you. This needs to encompass the key experiences that have shaped you, what matters most to you and the people you care about. In part I of this book we are laying down the foundation thinking. If you work your way through each page in sequential order, you will see why starting with the story of you matters. When you reach the conclusion of this book, you will clearly see why I am starting here. Let me direct your thinking to the current story of who you have been and who you are now.

I call this an 'I am...' statement.

## What is an 'I am...' statement?

For many years I (and my talented team) have been working with individuals (and organisations) around the world on the art of telling their story, of describing their 'self', their journey, their aspirations, their brand. The structure and methodology of an 'I am...' statement has proven to be a great way to support clients to write their story. Over and over, people tell us how the process of pulling together such a statement, of exploring themselves more deeply and honestly, leads to a profound desire to take action. From that foundation, people are in a much better position to start mapping out what's next.

So here we go...

The 'I am...' statement exercise provides an opportunity to step back and look at yourself to see who you really are. Trust me on this: to be able to share the story of you has real value for both you and those around you. Call it charisma or simply good communication, but being able to share your story helps others to honour what matters to you. (At the end of Chapter 2 I'll give you plenty of tips on how to share your story effectively.)

An 'I am...' statement gives you a structured and effective way to step out of the 'busy' and do the work on you. It's also sometimes referred to as a 'unique positioning' statement – 'unique' because no one else's statement will be the same as yours. Sure, there will be similarities and common experiences, but the skill is in how you interpret, write and then communicate your personal insights about what makes you uniquely you. So take a moment to be thoughtful about who you are and how you show up.

> *We don't see things as they are.*
> *We see things as we are.*
> **Anaïs Nin**

Your statement may be for you alone, to clarify your future direction and actions. Or it may have broader applications. If you are looking for a change in career or a promotion, this is an influential journey of self-discovery into the 'brand' of you. You'll discover what you are offering, where you are placed in your industry, and what your strengths and passions are. It's powerful to understand what your personality and behavioural traits are, and what the high-performing you looks like.

## The 'I am...' statement exercise

In formulating your statement, you will explore your so-called blind spots, some skewed or limiting beliefs you've picked up, skill deficits, values you think you hold but that you don't live and work by, things you wish for but don't work for, how different people in your life influence you and barriers to your greater success, happiness or empowerment.

This is a very personal, individual and reflective exercise. It's very much about letting go of your old worldview and seeing yourself with new eyes by really pondering the question, 'Who am I?' The process may require a new vulnerability; writing your story requires personal accountability for how you've been living your life.

The following activity, therefore, requires honesty and a genuine desire to work on you. As always, you will get out of it what you put into it. Be brave. Persevere through the uncomfortable bits. Keep remembering why you bought this book. Keep reading and start writing now!

## ʒthers how they view you

ιι ᷾ rising to discover how the various people in our lives describe ᷾ /for each will see us differently as a result of diverse experiences they have had with us. A lot of what others think is unknown to us; it may be quite surprising, shocking or exciting to reveal this.

Talking with people from all aspects of your life, and giving them permission to tell you their truth, can be disconcerting but it is super powerful. Listen actively and without judgment. Don't be defensive. Hear them out. Take notes and reflect later, when you're alone. Their honesty is your gift. I have seen people complete this process in so many creative ways. You could interview your children or set up a free online and anonymous survey. Remember you are an adult with your big girl or big boy pants on. You get to decide what you do with the feedback you receive.

Many people come up with a list of specific questions that they use to interview others, or they distribute the questions in written form. Examples of targeted questions include:

- Can you please describe me in five words?

- When is it hard to be around me?

- What value do you think I add to your life?

- What is your favourite memory of us?

- How do you feel when you think about our relationship?

- What do you trust about me?

- What do you think I need to pay attention to in my life?

- When are you most proud of me?

## Step 2 – Next, ask these questions of yourself

You will notice that these questions are about you as a whole person. They are not specific to your career or work history, because your identity is about so much more than the job you do. I'll talk more about that later.

- Who am I? (Write your answer in five sentences.)
- What do I most remember about my childhood?
- Which one person has most influenced me – how and why?
- What do I really want from life?
- How do I want to spend the rest of my life?
- What's it like being around me – at home, at work?
- What is important to me?
- What are my values and priorities?
- What makes me happy?
- What makes my heart hurt?
- What am I most proud of?
- What do I most want others to understand about me?
- What am I curious and thoughtful about?
- When I think about my future, what do I want the most?

**Do not answer these questions from a work perspective; rather, consider all aspects of your life.**

## Step 3 – Now spend time exploring the uniqueness of you

I can't tell you how often I talk about this with clients. Your uniqueness is your currency and greatest asset. It is essential that each and every one of us understands what we bring to the room. If you aren't clear about this, others won't be either. If you look around at your family, friends and peers at work, there is no other single person in the world who has got where they are because of the exact same experiences as you.

Sure, there are similarities and common moments we share with others, but being able to write and articulate the story of you requires that you can describe your originality. Why would a future employer choose you if you are the same as the person who was interviewed before you? This can be challenging to think about, but being able to answer these questions will potentially get you the next job, make your next date more meaningful, increase your self-awareness and undoubtedly contribute to success. If you can't answer the following questions now, come back to them after you have read through all the thought-provokers later in the book.

- How do I think differently to others?
- Can I describe my top three best attributes and how they add value to relationships?
- What makes me stand out from the crowd?
- What can I do brilliantly that people around me can't?
- What single life experience most changed me?
- What do others most appreciate about who I am?
- What evidence do I have to support my uniqueness?
- What do people consistently tell me I am amazing at?

## Step 4 – Think about your legacy

Legacies are not for old people! Every chapter of your life leaves a mark on the world. In this fourth step in thinking about your 'I am...' statement, we are going to explore what you want to be known and remembered for. Over the years, I have seen hundreds of 'I am...' statements. Years later I run into people and I don't necessarily remember their name, but I remember significant parts of their story and how I felt listening to them. Recently a man stopped me in the Sydney international airport. It had been six years since I watched him deliver his statement to his peers. I immediately asked him a question that related to his family and he responded with a teary smile.

People don't always remember who you work for or your job title, but they are likely to remember what you stand for and what matters to you. Read over what you've written in the first three steps and then answer the questions below. As you do, think of these questions as an accountability system. For example, if I want to be known as someone who is a 'trusted adviser', what did I do today to show people I can be trusted? Ask yourself:

- What do I want to be famous for?

- What do I want my family and friends to be most proud of me for?

- When I think about my funeral, what is it I want to be remembered for?

On page 181 you will bring the work you have done here, together with questions on writing and planning your next chapter.

> **Asking others, 'What's it like being around me?' is one of the most important questions you can ask when you are determining who you are in the world."**

## Chapter 2
# Do you understand your story?

You're now well into the groove of this book, and the sceptics, cynics and time-poor might be questioning the value of persevering. You obviously picked this book up because you're curious about getting your life in order or achieving success or finding fulfilment, but is it starting to feel a bit hard and uncomfortable?

Great! I'm doing my job.

So here's my next promise – it is worth your time to keep reading. But don't force it; just go with the flow, pick the book up, put it down – BUT DO PICK IT UP AGAIN.

Motivation fades and that's the normal for humans. But if you want something better, you need to commit and persevere. That's where success lies.

If you need a boost in motivation, read this chapter on the power and the rationale behind the 'I am...' statement. It's all about storytelling.

## Your story

Storytelling is a phenomenon that is fundamental to all nations, societies and cultures, and it has been so since time immemorial. It is a proven way to influence, inform and bond, and to build culture. Stories can explain and entertain, facilitate open and honest conversations, and build trust, compassion and understanding.

Organisations around the world are increasingly recognising that people are influenced at work by what's happening in other areas of their life. We are a whole person after all, and all our dots connect to tell our story.

---

**sto|ry** – *noun*

a narrative, either true or fictitious, in prose or verse, designed to interest, amuse or instruct

a narration of an incident or a series of events or an example of these as an anecdote, joke...

a narration of the events in the life of a person or the existence of a thing, or such events

a report or account of a matter; statement or allegation

---

Our story is our history, our present and our future. Stories help us express the how, what, when, where and why of who we are in a distinctive and personalised way, and they help us express what's important to us. Most of us more easily express our concerns, challenges and failings within the context of a prepared story.

You will never regret taking the time now to work out what it is that has most shaped who you are.

Storytelling is a step back in time, and yet a step forward in creating the future version of you. My work in organisations across the world has shown me that people who can tell their story are better able to persuade others to change their point

"Your story is uniquely yours. No other single human on this planet thinks, feels or looks the same as you. Your experiences, beliefs and values shape every decision you make!"

of view, and are also better at establishing rapport, credibility, authenticity and trust. If you live a life where other people play a significant part in your day, it's equally important to understand their story!

> *We become what we think about all day long.*
>
> **R. W. Emerson**

People like stories better than your CV, lectures, arguments, reporting, and facts and figures – and certainly better than just 'being told'. Skilled storytelling transforms uninspiring dialogue, diffuses tension, sparks up presentations and creates a more compelling picture of a leader's view or goals.

This is important. If you want to progress your career, inspire change in others or seek out the understanding of someone, give them the meaningful backstory of you. People connect most to how they feel when you are sharing, as opposed to what's actually being said.

Storytelling helps people share experiences, wisdom, knowledge, values, beliefs, insights, strength, hopes, goals and time. Stories help us to bond and befriend, to influence people and to share culture and history. When we hear a story that touches us, it's because that which matters has been transmitted. It takes hold of us; the storyteller's meaning has emerged and we feel a connection with, and receptivity to, the storyteller. There are lots of fancy strategies you can apply to creating success, but being a gifted storyteller is one of the most impactful skills I have observed in people.

Storytelling as a technique is easily adapted to handling the most intractable challenges, communicating who you are, enhancing your brand, transmitting your values, sharing your knowledge and leading people into the future.

Storytelling is part of the creative struggle to generate a new future. It enables us to move past all that makes sense and is logical and get to that realm where greater possibilities and deeper meaning are revealed. We all deserve this! We just need to do the work on understanding who we have been before and who we are now, and then we get to consciously choose how we will evolve.

 **Storytelling is a key skill for entrepreneurs and leaders; great storytelling is quick, powerful, refreshing, energising, collaborative, persuasive, holistic, entertaining, moving, memorable and authentic!"**

Storytelling satisfies the heart and both sides of the brain, and it is effective in building a faster emotional connection. Stories help connect all the dots, the rational and the emotional. For you to evolve and create change in your life, career and/ or relationships, you need people to be on the ride with you. With years of observing successful people under my belt, I can say this with confidence; none of them did it alone.

Storytelling frees us from our anchored perception of reality. When telling our own story, we are more authentic, open and vulnerable. Telling our story can reinforce our values and beliefs, remind us to do our best and that we can do more, be more and have more.

And we must embrace the reality of who we think we are compared to who others think we are. This can be annoying and embarrassing, or totally validating and beautiful. If you really struggle with the positive feedback and commentary of others, this is the time to say 'thank you' and own it.

Telling your own story creates an opportunity to build your profile and to articulate who you want to be and where you want to go, and what competencies you have to get there.

> **The story of you is the natural instrument of change and innovation, because it draws people in – to laugh, comment, act, think, talk, discuss, chat, joke, complain, dream, sympathise, agonise, enjoy, celebrate and understand YOU!"**

Stories hark back to our childhood and can interest, excite and delight us. When people are laughing and having a good time, they tend to let go of their normal scepticism and resistance and more willingly look at other perspectives and ideas.

Did I mention that storytelling is also fun? Well, I think it is. People fascinate me. I am that person who sits next to you on the plane and can't resist starting a conversation. When you go beneath the surface, everyone has something in their story for you to learn from. I am yet to meet someone who bores me. You just need to ask the right questions and listen, wholeheartedly. I can't begin to tell you how much of my learning has come from listening to people's stories.

## Reasons to embrace storytelling

In case you need some firm evidence that stories can change careers, relationships, learning and how we achieve success, here is a collection of quotes from the wise.

**Rick Levine, et al in *The Cluetrain Manifesto*:**

*Stories are much more compelling than information. Stories differ from information in that they have a start and a finish; they talk about events, not conditions; they imply a deep relationship among the events; stories are about particular humans; and stories are told in a human voice. As markets once again become conversations, marketers need to excel at telling compelling stories.*

**Mark Helprin:**

*The classic business story is much like the classic human story. There is rise and fall; the overcoming of great odds; the upholding of principles despite the cost; questions of rivalry and succession; and even the possibility of descent into madness.*

**James Bonnet:**

*Having lured us into the adventure by fantasies and a taste, the great story then provides us with a road map which is to say, it outlines all of the actions and tasks... we have to accomplish in order to complete one of these passages. Plus, it provides a tool kit for solving all of the problems that have to be solved to accomplish the actions and tasks... Every great story will divulge a little more of this truth, and bit by bit each step of the passage is revealed. Again, all of this is going on without the story recipient's conscious knowledge that it's happening.*

**Keith Johnstone:**

> *We were warned that algebra was going to be really difficult, whereas Einstein was told that it was a hunt for a creature known as 'X' and that when you caught it, it had to tell you its name.*

**John Seely Brown and Paul Duguid in *The Social Life of Information*:**

> *We tell stories because we have something exciting to tell. We tell stories to have fun, to entertain someone or keep them in suspense. We tell stories to let other people know what we're thinking. We tell stories to express our feelings. We tell stories to teach somebody something or to explain something. We tell stories to share ourselves to let other people get to know us better. We tell stories to give people enjoyment. We tell stories to get feelings out. We tell stories to use our imaginations. We tell stories to save our experiences forever.*

**Kieran Egan:**

> *Stories are linked beginning to end by the establishment of an expectation in the beginning that is satisfied in the end. Thus, good stories are characterised by a powerful principle of coherence. Stories hold their power over us as long as all the events stick to and carry forward the basic rhythm.*

**Peter Giuliano:**

> *Throw your mind wide open; let your emotions run free. We work so hard to think as opposed to feel and imagine, and you've got to allow yourself to feel and imagine. Most of life's decisions – personal decisions and business decisions – are driven by emotions. Regardless of the guilt or innocence of the person, the attorney whose opening argument is in the form of the best story invariably wins. Virtually every great leader has been a great storyteller. You've got to let your mind run free.*

## Top tips for sharing your story

I promised you some tips on how to share your story – if you want to and if it is beneficial. These work particularly well in the workplace.

1. **Own your story:** plan a way of sharing that makes *you* feel confident. Believe in you. Every single day of the life that you have lived has shaped who you are today. There is something that you are bringing to the room that is yours.

2. **Mind chatter is powerful:** avoid going to that place that assumes you will mess up or that people will poorly judge you. Assume your listeners are friendly, interested and supportive. Find the interesting story that people will want to listen to, a fresh take on you. Everyone has their more personal story – and just about everyone will feel out of their comfort zone in sharing it. Remember, there is strength in vulnerability.

3. **Calm your nerves:** if you are sharing your story with others (perhaps at work), think about the pre-sharing strategies that you can adopt. For example, before you start speaking, focus entirely on something else to distract yourself; alternatively, get into the 'zone' by blocking out everything else. Another tactic may be to stand tall, take deep breaths and 'put on' confident body language. Many people find it best to simply breathe slowly and deeply beforehand, consciously relaxing muscles, and then continue to manage their breathing and pauses once they start talking. (Great storytellers seem to average no more than 8 to 10 beats or syllables

between breaths, and rarely more than 12 – keep your breathing under control.) Manage your body language – tension is contagious. Remember, mostly people want you to do well. (There are sometimes doubters in the room but that's OK.) Acknowledge your nervousness; show your vulnerability – that's a powerful way to connect with your audience. Don't over-caffeinate! Sleep well the night before. Hydrate.

4. **Don't try to include too much:** for every point, ensure it earns its place in your allotted time. Is it interesting and is it helping people to know more of who you are? Avoid the obvious, such as things that people already know or can presume. Avoid anything boring – for example, content-rich PowerPoint slides, or a monotonous recounting of your life stages and experiences. Go deeper rather than broader – for example, it's not about listing all the places you've been but rather the impact on you of particular experiences. Focus on what is unique about you. Choose some key points about you and bring those to life.

5. **Think about structure:** this is the story of you so it needs to have a great opening line, be framed up, progress through a narrative and finish with 'punch'. For example, start by asking a question or presenting a problem, then describe the search for answers or a solution, and then bring it home with your most impactful points so your audience get the 'aha' moment. Aim to shift the audience's perspective of you in a meaningful way, so they 'know' you as they haven't known you before. Despite this advice, avoid sounding like you are following a formula or script – find your own natural and logical flow.

6. **Share your authentic story:** this is not just a description of you, and not just a list of places you've been and things you've done. What will people be interested to hear? How can you capture their attention? How can you interact with your listeners? What will make it worthwhile their listening? What will bring up some emotion? What problems, triumphs, sadnesses or people have *most* contributed to who you currently are? Have the courage to be more vulnerable than you usually are. Anecdotes should be explanatory or illustrative of something important. Humour is GREAT! Tears are OK!

7. **Plan your delivery:** if presenting to a group, will you have a set of points to cover, or a 'map' or graphics on slides, or will you memorise your talk? The latter is probably the ideal for a short talk, BUT only if you have prepared really well and feel confident about what you will say.

8. **Prepare well:** practise in front of a mirror and ideally in front of people. This does work! Remember that the quality of your content and your enthusiasm for the task of sharing your story are more important than a brilliant speaking style or slide deck. Everything I have seen in recent years tells me that people appreciate authenticity more than perfection.

9. **Connect with your audience:** make eye contact with every person. Start with those around the room who look most supportive and friendly, and then engage others. Think of your audience as friends you haven't seen for a while. The world is a mirror – put out the 'vibes' you want back.

10. **Use emotion:** allow your genuine emotions to enrich the experience for your listeners. Stories that trigger emotion are those that best inform, illuminate, inspire and move people. Tell your story with authenticity, courage and trust. Add some humour. Allow sadness if that is the authentic emotion. Show your passion and your enthusiasm for the things that are important to you. Your attitude is contagious – take your listeners on your journey and engage them.

11. **Use visual aids well – not as a crutch:** keep it simple. Don't use a slide deck as a substitute for notes or to read from, and use note cards only to prompt your next point. Use photos, video clips (60 seconds max), objects, maps and so on to bring interest to your talk. If you are using slides, consider restricting them to pictures or images – remember you're telling a story not giving a lecture. Skip text blocks and bullet points – aim for visual intrigue and images that add interest to what you are saying. Dress up, wear a hat or uniform, sing a song, play your guitar, display your trophy, show your loved ones. Bring your story to life.

12. **Vary your pattern of speech:** speak as you would in normal conversation. Think tone, pace and volume. Overall, a conversational style is better than oratory. Just be YOU. Use silence, pauses and questions to add dramatic effect. Give your audience an experience rather than just a talk, and a story rather than a lecture. What will the experience of listening to your story be like?

13. **Skip the ego:** no boasting, no victimhood (poor me), no distracting habits (swaying, fidgeting) and no jargon – this can be quite boring. A great presentation isn't about you sounding super smart. And, of course, be tasteful – there are some things best not disclosed. Be authentic, but use your better judgment.

Despite these tips, there is no best or perfect way. Use the tips as a guide but find your own rhythm. Above all, prepare and practise. This will give you a better chance of relaxing and enjoying telling your story.

I hope I've convinced you of the importance of being able to tell your story. But before you step on stage, you need to get really clear about your current state of being. You do this by taking a good hard look at yourself – the whole depth and breadth of you and your current situation. In doing this, you will come to a whole new level of understanding and awareness. And that's the topic of the next chapter.

# Chapter 3
# How self-aware are you?

We all assume we know ourselves best, right? Uhmm... maybe, sort of, yes. But indulge me here. Imagine your best friend is describing you, and now your mum, and next that guy who you cut in front of this morning in the traffic, and your boss, the neighbour, that person on your work team who doesn't like you, the nurse who cared for you in hospital, your school friend, your best friend, your worst enemy...

These people will all tell different stories of you. Does that mean some are wrong, untrue or inaccurate? Or are they all collectively the story you?

Remember the last time you decided to buy a car, and then looked for all the evidence to support that it was the right decision, and ignored what didn't 'fit'? Remember the last time you described something that happened, and you added your own bits to enhance the story? Remember when someone described you in a way that was just wrong?

And remember the last time you assumed something that turned out to be incorrect? What about the last time you sprouted the excuse rather than the truth (I couldn't do it because...). Or perhaps you blamed someone or something else because then you transferred 'fault' – you didn't have to take responsibility.

Get my drift? We often make things a bit 'wrong' for myriad reasons. We protect ourselves. We like to stay in our safe, comfortable zone. We don't particularly want to change – and we especially don't want to change something we've always believed. It can take just one comment to our childhood self to influence our thinking – forever – and it might be wrong!

## We're only human

'Experts' have said that in our humanness we get lots of stuff wrong, and yet we believe much of it to be true. Our perception of something becomes our reality, our truth. Hence, life – the world – is full of disagreement!

It can be hard to get away from our own presumed 'truth' and get to THE truth. And yet psychologists tell us we need that truth about ourselves, and that self-awareness, to be able to change and improve.

Self-awareness is a key component of emotional intelligence, which is a much greater indicator of success than intellectual intelligence. Do this work on you, and you will have your best chance at building the life you want.

Daniel Goleman's (1998) findings, and other research since, indicates that emotional intelligence contributes 80 to 90% of the competencies that distinguish *outstanding* leaders from *average* leaders. Think on that. Being 'smart' (your intellectual quotient or IQ) is a great advantage, but it is not 'enough' for great leadership and/or success.

Emotionally intelligent behaviours include:

- ► The ability to recognise and understand one's own moods, emotions and drivers as well as our effect on others.

- The ability to control or redirect disruptive impulses and moods and to think before acting.

- The passion to work for reasons beyond money or status; the propensity to pursue higher level goals with energy and persistence.

- The ability to understand the emotional makeup of other people and the skill of treating people according to their emotional reactions (as opposed to what words they say).

- Proficiency in managing relationships, building networks, finding common ground, building rapport and finding the 'lighter side' – the ability and desire to enjoy work and life and be an interesting, trustworthy and desirable person to be around.

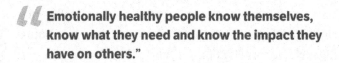

**Emotionally healthy people know themselves, know what they need and know the impact they have on others."**

So what is the prerequisite to more emotionally intelligent behaviour?

Self-awareness.

Know that you *can* improve your emotional intelligence; you can learn the behaviours of emotionally intelligent people. The first step is building self-awareness – knowing where you are now and gaining clarity on what you need to learn and change to improve this skill. You will see that these questions build further on the work you started in step 2 of the 'I am...' statement activity. These questions might hurt your head and even feel somewhat philosophical, but they aren't. These are questions I explore in coaching sessions all the time. If you can't answer these authentically and with clarity, you are limiting how others understand you.

Critically, people will find it hard to support you with next steps. So take some time to stop here. The benefits of this work will come later.

- What do you know about you?
- What do you not know about you?
- What do others know about you?
- What do others not know about you?
- What do you want others to know about you?

Think about who you really are – at work, at home and in the community. Take this opportunity to develop an honest, comprehensive and holistic view of you. Gather as much information as possible to come to a greater self-awareness; to identify what distinguishes you from others, and what makes you uniquely you.

## Biases

If you are interested in some theory, here is a just a little of what we coaches understand about why biases impact our state of being so much.

**Myside bias** (also called confirmatory bias) is a tendency for people to favour information that confirms their precon- ceptions, regardless of whether the information is true. As a result, people gather evidence and recall information from memory selectively and interpret it in a biased way. Hang in here with me. If your eyes are glazing over, keep in mind that this section of the book explains *why* you think and feel the way you do.

The biases appear, in particular, for emotionally significant issues and for established beliefs. For example, in reading about gun control, which is such a big issue around the world right now, people usually seek out sources of information that affirm their existing attitudes. They are, no doubt, aware of an opposing view, but they rely on and defer to information that supports their bias. They also tend to interpret ambiguous evidence as supporting their existing position.

This process of 'biased searching', interpretation and/or recall have been invoked to explain:

► **Attitude polarisation** – when a disagreement becomes more extreme even though the different parties are exposed to the same evidence.

► **Belief perseverance** – when beliefs persist after the evidence for them is shown to be false.

► **The irrational primacy effect** – a stronger weighting for data encountered earlier on.

► **Illusory correlation** – in which people falsely perceive an association between two events or situations.

Research suggests that people are biased towards confirming their existing beliefs. (And why wouldn't they be? It's much more uncomfortable to challenge our existing beliefs, right?) We tend to test ideas in a one-sided way, focusing on one possibility and ignoring alternatives. In combination with other effects, this strategy can bias the conclusions that are reached.

Explanations for the observed biases include wishful thinking and the limited human capacity to process information. Another suggestion is that people show confirmation bias because they are pragmatically assessing the costs of being wrong, rather than investigating in an objective way.

Confirmation biases contribute to overconfidence in personal beliefs and can maintain or strengthen faulty or limiting beliefs even in the face of contrary evidence.

Translation: in other words, if people ever use words like arrogant or stubborn to describe you, go back and read this chapter again. You are not always right and, anyway, why does being right even matter? Later we'll discuss picking your battles.

## Beliefs

A belief is simply a thought that you have had before that you continue to think. But never underestimate the power of them. Our beliefs determine the way we think, feel, behave, interact with others, work and live.

So, you need to understand your beliefs – where they came from and why – and challenge yourself to find out if they are actually assumptions about something, rather than *the* truth.

Open your mind to other possibilities and the 'truth' of other people's perceptions. Open the way for more disclosure, greater transparency and a desire for honest feedback. Then incorporate any new self-knowledge into your belief system, and act on it.

## ✐ Activity

What beliefs do you currently hold (about yourself) that might not be *true*?

_____

_____

_____

_____

What might others (wrongly or inaccurately) believe about you?

_____

_____

_____

_____

What beliefs do you currently hold that limit you? For example, any self-talk that starts with, 'I can't... I won't... I shouldn't... I'm not good at... I've always... I never...'

_____

_____

_____

_____

What assumptions have you made about the impact you have on others?

_____

_____

_____

_____

How can you find out what you might wrongly or inaccurately believe?

_____

_____

_____

_____

What beliefs do you have that serve you?

_____

_____

_____

_____

What beliefs do you have that get in the way of your success?

_____

_____

_____

_____

## Values

Your values are your principles or standards of behaviour, and your judgment about what is important in life. Your values are, therefore, an important component in the story of you.

As with beliefs, your values are mostly laid down in your early years and are then refined and re-shaped throughout your life. They affect how you think, feel, live, relate, interpret, decide things and respond/react. A misalignment between what you value and how you are living and working can be stressful and unsatisfying.

People often connect values with a *sense of purpose*. If you think about any conflict that's happening in your life, it's probably the result of a conflict in values. Our values show themselves in every interaction, decision and relationship. Do you know what yours are?

## ✎ Activity

What do you *most* value, what is *most* important to you?

Simply tick the five words in the list below that best represent your personal core values. This list is far from complete; add any others that are particularly important for you.

| | | |
|---|---|---|
| ☐ Accomplishment | ☐ Excellence | ☐ Originality |
| ☐ Accountability | ☐ Fairness | ☐ Ownership |
| ☐ Acknowledgment | ☐ Faith | ☐ Participation |
| ☐ Adventure | ☐ Focus | ☐ Passion |
| ☐ Authenticity | ☐ Free spirit | ☐ Peace |
| ☐ Beauty | ☐ Freedom | ☐ Performance |
| ☐ Boldness | ☐ Fun | ☐ Perseverance |
| ☐ Challenge | ☐ Growth | ☐ Productivity |
| ☐ Collaboration | ☐ Happiness | ☐ Recognition |
| ☐ Commitment | ☐ Healthy living | ☐ Relationships |
| ☐ Community | ☐ Honesty | ☐ Respect |
| ☐ Comradeship | ☐ Humour | ☐ Risk taking |
| ☐ Confidentiality | ☐ Imagination | ☐ Romance |
| ☐ Connectedness | ☐ Independence | ☐ Safety |
| ☐ Contribution | ☐ Integrity | ☐ Self-expression |
| ☐ Creativity | ☐ Justice | ☐ Sensitivity |
| ☐ Curiosity | ☐ Knowledge | ☐ Spirituality |
| ☐ Directness | ☐ Learning | ☐ Success |
| ☐ Discovery | ☐ Love of family | ☐ To be known |
| ☐ Efficiency | ☐ Love of self | ☐ Tradition |
| ☐ Empowerment | ☐ Nurturing | ☐ Trust |
| ☐ Equality | ☐ Orderliness | ☐ Winning |

Now consider where your particular values came from. How did they develop? Who most influenced you as a child? What beliefs underpin your values? Are these beliefs faulty? Would you prefer to be living different values? If so, what would you need to change?

 **Values are like fingerprints. Nobody's are the same, but you leave them all over everything you do."**

Critically reflect on this – are you living in line with these core values? For example, if your family is your number one priority, do you live up to that and give them the best of yourself? If your health is a high priority, do you eat, sleep, exercise and take care of yourself well?

Just as important is being aware of the values that are *least* important to you. You may like to underline these five words in the preceding list too.

## Don't f**k it up! Self-sabotage is rife!

Over and over again, I've seen people walk through the doors of my coaching practice who display particular behaviours and attitudes that absolutely get in the way of them achieving success.

You are a complex human who can be prone to making dumb-ass decisions (yes, insert laughing here) and, as a result, you have full permission to make mistakes and not get it right all the time. However, from my observation, I have noticed that there are common patterns of behaviour that we tend to adopt when we feel pressured. Take some time to reflect on your past. When it went wrong, why did it go wrong? There are always going to be influences that are not in our control, but the way we think, behave, feel and make choices IS in our control.

Patterns of behaviour are challenging to alter. But being self-aware and catching yourself in the moment means you're halfway to making a positive change. If you can identify the behaviours and circumstances under which you tend to fold, you will be more able to sidestep and make a different choice.

Please be clear here that I am talking about self-sobatage. You should absolutely be making mistakes and messing things up sometimes, because that means you are trying new things and have opportunities for learning.

Here are my top 15 'I am going to sabotage myself' behaviours to look out for (and avoid!):

1. **People pleasing** – it's exhausting and rarely works as a strategy.

2. **Hanging out with energy vampires** – they suck the life out of you.

3. **Overthinking** – it doesn't get results.

4. **Listening to the devil on the shoulder** – look for the angel instead.

5. **Making fear-based decisions** – pushing through the fear is where the joy is.

6. **Living in the past** – that chapter has closed; it's time for a new one.

7. **Compromising your values for others** – this is your life so live it aligned with what matters to you.

8. **Comparing yourself to others** – this gets you nowhere fast.

9. **Believing others make you 'feel' a certain way** – you are responsible for your own feelings.

10. **Being your own worst critic** – constructive criticism is OK, berating yourself is not.

11. **Starting things on a Monday** – what's wrong with today?

12. **Expecting things to change when you won't** – why would they?

13. **Feeling guilty about things that don't matter** – don't feign guilt to justify your inaction.

14. **Thinking like a victim** – you aren't what happened to you so take responsibility.

15. **Believing your own excuses** – make an effort not an excuse.

If you are really committed to f**king up, just keep on doing what doesn't work. If you are committed to making positive change, be aware, take a moment and make another choice.

You really are the creator of your next chapter. You get to decide where you are going to go!

# Part II
## Thought-provokers

*It's time to start living the life*
*you imagined.*

**Henry James**

t's time to pay attention and grab a pen. It's time to be
responsible for you. You will never regret dedicating time
to work on you.

Think of this second part of the book as a personal
coaching session. Here you'll find what I call thought-
provokers (or TPs) – and there are 20 of them. They are all the
hot topics that I have repeatedly discussed as a success coach
over two decades – and no doubt will continue to discuss as
long as I continue to do this work!

# Success (whatever that means)

**The secret to success in three words – *do the work!***

You'll find that throughout this book you'll be required to think; to think some more and then to take action.

One important thing to think about is what 'success' means to you. Success means different things at different times to each of us. Some people never feel successful and others are very clear about what they need to have and feel to claim success. Put simply, it is important that we create a vision of where we are heading.

You'll notice that while you're thinking, there's space on these pages for you to record your thoughts. So review the questions and jot down your thoughts in the spaces provided. Haven't got a pen? Not sure what to write? Come on – remember the secret to success? You'll need to do the work!

My point is that whatever you want to create, or 'be' more or less of, is what we will work on here. Don't get hung up on words like success and what they are meant to mean. Other people's perceptions don't count here.

Drill down to what you really want. Do you want to be healthier, happier, wealthier, smarter? Why? Perhaps you want to change your career, or start or end a relationship? Why? More specifically, what will you gain?

You might be considering starting a new business or be working up to a promotion. There could be a big adventure you want to plan or maybe it's time to go back and do some study. It might be you'd like something small or something that will literally change your life and how you live it.

For some people, success is exercising twice per week and being able to pay all their bills; for others, it is running a marathon each year and having a loving relationship.

I do warn you here to consider how much you associate success with material things. Often people talk to me about success in a way that is connected with lifestyle and money. How happy will you be on your yacht if you are on it alone? It's also really important to be able to be happy with your current self in your current life, until you get 'there'. Hang on tight to the people who matter as you create change. It's your job now to do the work on you, and to invest the hours and effort in bringing your dreams, plans and changes to life. I am certain that the people who are most successful in life are those who have absolute clarity on what success will look and feel like when they get there.

When writing this book, I thought about success a lot. In case it's of interest to you, I personally link success closely with my ability to be resilient and adapt to what's happening around me. I feel successful when the people I love have what they need from me. I know more success will come for me if I learn, evolve, get uncomfortable, plan and do the work!

Another part of how I measure success is by how much people trust me. So what I do is what I say I am going to do. Success is also knowing I can pay the bills and travel. I asked my 12 year old what success means to him and he said, 'It's how it feels when you mark the ball in footy, mum.' I love that he connected success with an experience and a feeling, as opposed to a thing!

## Don't be afraid of your awesomeness

The talented Marianne Williamson, bestselling author and spiritual teacher, nailed it when she wrote:

> *Our deepest fear is not that we are inadequate. Our deepest fear is that we are powerful beyond measure. It is our light not our darkness that most frightens us. We ask ourselves, 'Who am I to be brilliant, gorgeous, talented, and fabulous?' Actually, who are you NOT to be?... Your playing small does not serve the world.*

Williamson claimed there is nothing to be gained by shrinking yourself so that others around you don't feel insecure. She feels we are all meant to shine, as children do... 'It is not just in some of us, it is in everyone.'

## The bottom line on success

- ► Let's not play small in this life.
- ► Let's determine our own version of success.
- ► Let's not wait for the right time or circumstance.
- ► It's time to explore our potential.
- ► It's time to be brilliant – to shine.
- ► Our future is calling.
- ► Let's be resolute, committed and courageous.

# Coaching Questions

1. Is success the same as happiness?

2. Can I be happy but not successful?

3. Can I be successful but not happy?

4. When do I feel most successful?

5. What does success look like for me?

6. How will I know if I'm leading my most successful life?

7. What do I tell others about what success means to me?

8. Can I specifically write out what I will be doing when I've created my version of success? Do it here!

9. Who will be by my side?

## TP #2

# This was not my plan

**Life is largely about how we handle the stuff that goes wrong!**

I hear from my clients over and over some version of, 'This was not my plan', followed with some version of, 'I never expected this', and 'I don't know what to do' or 'I feel stuck in this situation'.

Let me tell you, no one is planning their divorce on their wedding day. And I haven't met anyone yet who has a strategy for becoming overweight. I've also not come across anybody who looks forward to redundancy or having a sick child. Not too many of us get through life without heartbreak, pain, loss and unplanned events.

We could frame these moments as learning opportunities, but that just sounds like cringe-worthy self-help speak.

Alternatively, we can just get on with writing a new plan for moving forward. But don't overthink this! You can always let it evolve as you progress. It doesn't need to look pretty or perfect. Think of this as brainstorming. The main thing is to get started and to take this first step.

So, what do you need to think about, feel and let go of before you can make a specific, new, achievable plan?

Start writing notes now – anywhere in these pages, or grab a notebook.

## Coaching Questions

**1** Do I know what I really want?

**2** What decisions would I make if I trusted my instincts, believed in myself, backed myself, took time for myself?

**3** What is possible for me now? (Think big but in small increments or steps.)

**4** What decisions/actions most need my attention? (What are my priorities?)

**5** What can I implement immediately?

**6** What do I know I need to do differently?

**7** What is in my control? And what do I need to let go of?

**8** Will I be better, stronger, smarter and more self-aware when I make and implement this plan?

**9** What have I always wanted to do, but not done?

**10** Does my plan reflect my passions, strengths and values?

It's funny (not really) how we still do things we know aren't good for us and we get 'stuck' on questions that don't help us move forward. These questions can be both disempowering and victim-like. I've given them a good try out myself but, nope, nothing good comes from them.

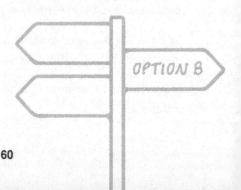

**Be mindful where you invest your energy and catch yourself if these questions keep coming up because they are often NOT helpful at all:**

- **Why did this happen to me?**
- **What did I do wrong?**
- **Will it happen again?**
- **Why is life so unfair?**

## Activity

Write down what you want to change: the specific few things you will stop, start and continue.

Identify what you will create: what success will look and feel like.

Identify the barriers and how you will push through them.

Outline what you need to commit to, how you will persevere through the hard times and what you will hold fast to – your non-negotiables.

*My plan* _____

_____

_____

_____

_____

_____

_____

_____

_____

# I am my most important project

**The world is full of people who start stuff.**
**Be the opposite of that!**

Imagine if we treated the plan for our life as if it were our most important project. When we watch high potential individuals plan projects at work, they put significant time into considering the goals they want to achieve. They do a full audit on all the data available, they consult experts and they identify opportunities. They conduct a risk assessment and make strategic and thoughtful decisions before implementation. They review as they progress and they commit.

It sounds like a pretty boring process I know, but the point is that if you took the same amount of care planning your life as you do those professional projects, things would be different. The purpose of this book is to help you do that, by making YOU your most important project. Investing in YOU is the most important investment you will ever make.

The first time I thought about this was a real light-bulb moment for me. I literally made a collage – a strategic plan sounds more impressive, but it was really a poster of all the things I wanted to create, do and build. I needed a visual on my 'life project'. I'll share the elements of this project here with you now:

- I knew I wanted to one day buy a home for my children.

- I had a dream to buy a beach box.

- I really wanted to travel to Italy with my family.

- I wanted a self-sustaining business doing meaningful work – this was critical in my version of success.

- I knew having a healthy mind and body would sit at the core of my new life.

Once I had the visual representation, I then wrote out exactly what was required of me to bring this to life. I detailed everything from who I would seek advice from to the timelines I wanted to commit to. I showed it to people and sought their advice. I adapted it as I evolved. This was the project of me. To this day, nearly nine years later, I still spend time talking with my coaching clients about how they will make themselves their most important project.

So make a cup of tea (or pour a wine), get out your notepad and really invest some time into auditing your life right now.

Part of making your plan is understanding what you want and why. Some refer to this as 'purpose'; some would simply ask: 'What makes you happy?'

Let's not overcomplicate this – just write down what your goals are (if you didn't in the previous section) and keep building on your notes as you go. I'll keep asking some of the same questions because you may change your thinking as you gain more insight.

# Coaching Questions

**1** What are my goals? Are they specific enough?
Have I drilled down to the most meaningful goals?

**2** What timeframes do I already know I need to set?
(Keep these realistic.)

**3** Who else do I need to involve/consult? What support
will I need?

**4** What might get in the way of my success?

**5** What do I know will be hard?

**6** What can I start doing today?

**7** What ideas haven't I thought of yet?

**8** What opportunities could I explore now?

**9** How committed am I to my goals?

**10** How will I keep myself accountable for doing what
I mean to do?

**11** What will be required of me financially, emotionally
and physically?

**12** What compromises am I prepared to make?

**13** How will I look after myself during project me?

## TP #4
# Doing what's required

**Start by doing what is necessary, then what is possible, and suddenly you are doing the impossible.**

**Francis of Assisi**

It's easy to be awesome when life is easy. But what about when it's hard? It doesn't seem fair that when we are most challenged we have to be at our strongest. But that is the reality, so let's get on with it.

So many of us START so many things. We start diets, we start exercise plans, we start new relationships, we start study, we start businesses, we start being kinder, we start writing a book... But how many of us finish the things that create change and success?

Adults are bad at change.

We don't like it.

It's uncomfortable.

It's annoying.

It's easier to stay the same.

So, here's me, challenging you...

Doing what's required means I will take action even when I don't want to. Even when I'm tired or it's too hot or I feel lazy and my children have been vomiting with gastro the night before, I will do it anyway.

## " Successful people do what others aren't prepared to do."

Like everyone else, successful people still have things to learn and things get in their way BUT they are successful because they don't wait. They don't give in. Their tantrums are short-lived.

When we do what's required, we also get what I call 'accidental development'. If you take a step every day towards your goals, you will find you are learning, growing and developing.

I had a rather hilarious conversation with a friend of mine who is a published author. I remember flippantly and excitedly telling him that I was going to write a book. 'It will be so much fun,' I said. 'Not really,' he replied.

He outlined the process of writing a book, the hours of thinking, deleting, proofing, re-writing and eyestrain. I clearly remember him telling me that you get to know the content so well that you can't remember if you've written it or where you've put it and you start writing it again. That when you are proofing, you can't then recall if you've already read that bit in another chapter.

Oh, how I laughed at the ridiculousness of that. After talking with him, I knew that there would be hours of work, TV missed, late nights, frustration and huge, joyful satisfaction in the process.

Then he looked at me and asked, 'Are you really prepared to do what's required to write a book?' From memory my reply was, 'Mmm I'll have to think about that.' So I did and here we are.

I regularly have coaching clients tell me that they want to step into entrepreneurship, take all their experience and develop their own business. Great! Do you know what it is I then ask them? (insert smiling here): 'Do you know what it will take to do that and are you prepared to do what's required?' Sometimes the answer is no. Here are some questions to support your thinking.

## Coaching Questions

**1** What is my commitment, on a scale from 1 to 10?

**2** Am I really prepared to do what I know I need to do to be successful?

**3** Will I do the work every day?

**4** Will I involve others to keep me accountable?

**5** Can I describe and visualise what success will look like?

**6** Do I feel absolutely committed to making the required changes?

**7** Do I have strategies in place to create momentum?

**8** What are the consequences of me doing what's required?

**9** How does this fit with my life plan?

**10** How will it feel to make this happen?

**11** What would happen if I let this go?

## TP #5
# Unlearn

**It is impossible for anyone to begin to learn that which one thinks one already knows.**
**Epictetus**

Yes, to 'unlearn' is an actual thing!

It's said that once you've had a thought six times it becomes your belief! A bit simplistic, I know, but the point is that once you believe something, your brain looks for evidence to prove you're right – remember I discussed 'myside bias' back in part I? What we habitually perceive and believe and find 'proof' for becomes our reality and what we live by.

Compounding that, research indicates (simplistically) that 95% of the thoughts we have today, we will have again tomorrow. So we're continually, habitually, going about our day, evidence-gathering to make our previous learning right. And some of it goes back to our earliest childhood.

Do you know that you probably even have a routine when you shower? We travel to work in the most efficient way each day and we tend to attract friends who think just like us. As adults, we get very attached to being right, whereas children are so great at learning and unlearning. The normal outcome is that we believe some things to be true that, in fact, are not true!

The current 'busy' lifestyle that many of us are leading does not give us the time it takes to think about this. But you bought the book and here we are, so let's think about this now! Awesome.

Here I am, challenging you (again)!

 **We think our belief is the truth."**

What do you need to unlearn? Most likely, you have many thoughts and behaviours that really don't serve you well – either for where you are right now or where you want to go. Some beliefs you hold will be wrong and some will be limiting you: think about all your 'I can't/don't/won't' thinking, and all your 'I'm not good at' or 'This is just the way I am' self-judgments.

For a moment, give yourself permission to regress into your childhood self, before the world took the shine off you; when you were an open book and open-minded; when you thought the best of you and the world was a big exciting place and you wanted to experience and know it all. Go back to when you were a sponge for new learning and when learning was fun. Remember learning to ride a bike, growing a tadpole, going to a new place; when you asked a million questions and learned a million things – every day.

Or maybe tap into your rebellious, teenage self. Remember when you questioned everything and disagreed for the sake of it; when a priority was to get away from rules, restrictions and the judgment of others and experience life on your own terms? Remember when you took risks? Maybe you protested, or saved whales, or joined a political party or smoked a joint.

Or maybe go back to when you were first madly, happily in love. When you believed in all the good in the world and that being loveable and happy was your due.

Just let yourself go there for a while. Challenge everything you think you now know. Ask lots of 'why' questions. Consider others' opinions. Read a book. Listen more. Reflect on beliefs you hold. There are things you learnt from your parents, teachers, co-workers and others – years ago – that are so ingrained in your thinking that you aren't even aware of the influence they have on your decision-making and your relationships today.

# Coaching Questions

**1** What am I thinking that may not be true?

**2** What habitual thoughts do I have that don't serve me?

**3** Do I think less of me than I should because others judged me (or I judged myself) too harshly?

**4** What strategies have I learnt as an adult that really don't work?

**5** Are there negative or limiting thoughts that aren't even mine, which I've never challenged or reflected on or re-assessed?

**6** Have I thoughtlessly fallen into a 'culture' – a way of doing and being?

**7** When was the last time I had a brand-new thought, something I'd never thought before?

**8** Have I recently thought of a question that I really don't know the answer to?

**9** Am I taking responsibility for who I am being and what more I need to learn?

**10** What is a different way?

**11** How would someone else respond to this?

**12** What do I need to unlearn?

# TP #6
# Motivation versus commitment

**Motivation happens on the inside and for a moment. Commitment is what you do even when you don't want to.**

This is very annoying to think about, but please stay with me here. Many of us grew up associating the word 'motivation' with all things positive. 'Motivational speakers' are amazing, right? Motivation is something that successful people do well, isn't it? Being self-motivated is a strength, right?

I once read a book just on the benefits of motivation. I hate to be a party pooper (do people still say that?), but in my years working as a success coach it's been really obvious to me that motivation fades. It's great – but it's fleeting and inconsistent and unreliable.

How many of us start something on a Monday, like a diet, and by Wednesday we are eating four slices of peanut butter toast because we're hungry? Or we have vowed to ask for a promotion, yet back away when the manager looks too busy.

The behaviour/mindset/skill that gives us the greatest chance of success is commitment. So that even if we eat the toast, breaking our no-carb rule, and delay seeing the manager one day because we are procrastinating, we gather ourselves and get back on the case the next. We are committed to the end goal and to persevering.

I have a client who rocked my world. Let's call him Darrel because that's his name. He grew up in a small town in New Zealand. He was the little blue-eyed boy who couldn't read in his early schooling years, but he was the man who would teach himself to swim and go on to complete numerous triathlons.

What? Yes! I remember him deciding that he would go out into the bay and teach himself freestyle (as you do). Of course, his motivation was high because he is a naturally self-driven and rather extraordinary individual, but the reason for his success was his commitment.

When he missed waking up with his children on a Sunday morning due to his training schedule, he found another way to connect with them. When it was cold and raining, he went running, swimming and cycling anyway. His muscles would hurt and his brain would scream at him to stop. It was his commitment to the end goal that kept him focused. When the motivation passed, his vision and the training plan he committed to, kept him on track. He knew his non-negotiables and what he needed to do to succeed, and that was what he did. He never talked to me about feeling motivated. Darrel talked to me about his commitments.

 **Motivation is a feeling; commitment is a mindset."**

Commitment means you do it when you want to AND when you don't want to. When the motivation has passed, it is commitment that holds you accountable.

Spend some time just thinking about when you have been truly committed to something and what you achieved.

Reflect on what you were doing consistently.

When you have finished patting yourself on the back, move on to the questions.

## Coaching Questions

**1** When have I been successful before and what behaviours did I demonstrate?

**2** What am I already committed to in my life? (What's working?)

**3** When has motivation let me down? (Reflect and learn.)

**4** How can I integrate higher-level commitment into my planning and thinking (so that I am not dependent on motivation)?

**5** What would be different for me if I were committed?

**6** How can I seek the support of others to hold me accountable?

## TP #7

# Honouring the future you

**Your imagination is the preview to life's coming attractions.**
**Albert Einstein**

Oh geez, with each year I get older and wiser. I can't believe people actually paid to hear me speak ten years ago. My life experience was so limited back then. What were they thinking? But that's the reality, isn't it? Imagine you in two years' time and how much more you will know in five years' time, and in ten years you will be so wise (please note, that's NOT the same as 'old').

So, when I am making big decisions or creating change, I wonder what the future smarter/wiser/funnier/more experienced version of me would tell me to do now.

Do you have a clear vision of your future self?

My experience as a success coach clearly shows me that when we can imagine it, we are far more likely to achieve it. I knew I wanted to take my children out of school and travel to Italy for a period of time. I could actually visualise, draw, write and describe what it would be like waking up in Rome. I knew what needed to happen before we would get there, and I knew that I trusted the future version of me to be adventurous enough to make this a reality. I talked about the Italy trip well before I had the plan in place, or the money saved, because I was honouring the future me.

Your vision can evolve and change over time, of course, but can you imagine yourself in the future? Consider what noise/pain/anger/resentment you could let go of so that your future self doesn't have to carry it. People who are emotionally healthy are good at letting stuff go. Your future self will thank you for the work you do on yourself now.

There are people all around the world with less experience and knowledge than you living your greatest ambitions, because they believed in themselves and told others to.

**❝❝ The best way to predict your future is to live it now."**

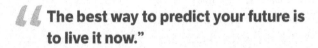

## Coaching Questions

**1** What am I really great at now that I will build on?

**2** What have my greatest life lessons been that serve me now?

**3** What did I waste time worrying about in the past?

**4** What advice does my future self have for me now?

**5** What do I need to let go of?

**6** What would my future self challenge me on?

**7** Can I describe/imagine my future self?

**8** Do I like my future self and why?

# Saying yes

**When you are saying yes to others, make sure you aren't saying no to something that matters more.**

This is important: everything you say YES to means you are potentially saying NO to something else. Please note here that this is not just a challenge for people-pleasers. Many of us say yes to things because of what feel like really valid reasons. It might be that saying yes to that request means a possible promotion or helping someone who we know really needs it. This thought-provoker is very much about raising your awareness of whether you are saying yes to the things that will serve you now and later.

I always laugh on the inside (and sometimes on the outside) when people ring and ask me if I can come and speak to their people about time management. What's to manage? You actually can't manage time. There are 24 hours in the day and, as far as I know, it's staying that way. A better way to think about it is to consider what you will do with your 24 hours.

For example, when you say YES to that client dinner, you are saying NO to your family. When you say YES to exercise, you are saying NO to a heart attack (that might be overly dramatic, but you know what I mean). Maybe your choice works out well, or maybe there's a consequence you didn't think about and didn't want.

When we are clear about what matters to us, we can prioritise. We more consciously choose to invest time in things that pay us back and that work for us, such as energy, health, relationships and quality of life.

There's a term we use in the coaching world: the opportunity cost. A question I commonly ask people is, 'What will it cost you to do that?' The cost might be financial, emotional, social or physical.

Every time you say YES to a commitment, and you use up some of your time, it costs you with either negative or positive impacts. Sometimes the cost is immediate; other times it happens down the track.

For example, writing this book cost me 250 hours of time; time away from my children, from other work, from income-producing events, from social opportunities and so on. But that feels great, because I know the positive impact it will have. I'm consciously choosing to make this book come to life, and I'm happy to pay the price. Do you see my point here?

## *ʺ* Know what matters and say yes to that."

Catch yourself in conversations and when you're entering something into your calendar, and think about the cost. Are you prepared to pay it? It can be really helpful to come up with language you can use when you want to say no but feel the need to say yes; for example, 'I wish I could help with that but I'm working to a tight deadline today.'

Use your time well and mindfully. You only have today once.

It becomes easier to say NO when you have clarity on this.

## Coaching Questions

1. Am I doing what I want to do and what is right for me at this time?

2. If I look in my calendar for the next four weeks, what (or who) should I have said no to?

3. What consequences are playing out for me by saying yes too often?

4. What stops me from saying no more often?

5. Do I need to learn more ways to say no?

6. What do I want to say yes to that I haven't?

7. What do I want to say no to that I haven't?

8. Where can I create space for the things that matter most?

9. Will I more consciously choose where I allocate my time from today?

## TP #9
# Resilience over happiness

**Do not judge me by my successes. Judge me by how many times I fell and got back up again.**
**Nelson Mandela**

I feel there has been so much hype in recent years around the concept of happiness. Here's my take: we don't need to be happy all the time, and if we're not happy it doesn't mean we are sad. I know! Breaking news.

Life is all shades of grey (and I am not referencing any weird sexual stuff here). A full life encompasses it all, the gamut of emotions, the plethora of feelings and the richness of emotional experience – OK, getting dramatic again, but you get my drift. Love, fear, joy, sadness, surprise, anger – that's life!

I believe happiness is an outcome... stay with me on this. Here's what I have observed in my own life and in 99% of the lives of the successful people I have coached. (I made that number up but I think it would be pretty close if tested.)

Happiness is a consequence of how we manage what happens, and it's the people who have resilience who are happiest. The people who 'bounce back' better and faster spend less time down and more time up – that's logical, right?

*Courage is optional.*

**Craig Harper**

## The bottom line on happier people

- ► Have a greater ability to 'reframe'; to look for the positive, the solution, the better response, the bigger picture, the best way out or forward.
- ► Get their own ego out of the way and see beyond their initial 'default', self-focused reaction.
- ► Don't stay long in victimhood, or look to allocate blame or inflict punishment – rather, they step out of the human drama gracefully.
- ► Still feel the more negative emotions, but more quickly move on.
- ► Manage their response rather than just go with the situation. They choose courage.

People who take responsibility for themselves and their own decisions and actions are the happiest. And happier people spend most time with others who are optimistic and happy, and minimal time with people who drag them down – emotions are catchy things!

In my experience, people who are resilient in their responses to what life throws at them are more peaceful and healthier – physically, emotionally and spiritually. They're happier, though they do not need to be happy all the time.

The good news is that I have worked with enough people to know that all these behaviours and attitudes that happier people display can be learned.

The smarty-pants people call this emotional intelligence (we talked about this in part I).

# Coaching Questions

**1** What would happen if I spent more time thinking about how to build resilience, instead of how to be happy – if I saw resilience (and, therefore, happiness) as a skill I can learn?

**2** What are the benefits to me if I am more resilient?

**3** Am I ready to work on me – to find out more about the behaviours of emotionally intelligent people so that I may start practising these behaviours?

**4** Am I prepared to identify opportunities that will build my resilience?

**5** Am I ready to work on me, to put in the effort to move away from default responses, and concentrate more on responses that will get me to a happier place?

**6** How would I need to think differently? What mindset shifts would I need to make?

**7** How would I need to behave/respond differently?

## TP #10
# Do not play small

**Your playing small does not serve the world.**
Marianne Williamson

Your life is a direct reflection of what you think of you.

Over and over again, I hear people minimising their strengths and ambitions – being modest. They don't want to sound arrogant or self-promoting, or become subject to the 'tall poppy' syndrome. I also see people who have fallen into the habit or a culture of comfort – giving less and doing the same thing over and over because that is easier. And I see people putting a low priority on their own needs and ambitions as they run that treadmill that is life.

Research tells us that people leave 60% of their potential at home. That means on any given day, if you were really 'in the zone' you could do much better by being the very best version of you. OMG! Imagine what you are really capable of, and what you could achieve, if you set your mind to it.

There can be valid reasons for people making conservative decisions. There are times when we are risk-averse in our approach. Maybe we have financial challenges or a relationship that needs attention. Perhaps our confidence has taken a knock. But if you are reading this book, hopefully it's because you are done with playing small. Congratulations.

Successful people aren't the smartest or the best educated – they're the ones who think big and act. Playing big in the world is a way of being; where language, choices and experiences are all different. Change is essential. Setbacks are inevitable. It won't be easy – but it will definitely be worth it!

## The bottom line on playing big

- ► Saying YES to uncertainty and discomfort.
- ► You are ready to get yourself out there in the game of life, so give it your best shot, be courageous and back yourself.
- ► You will own your ambitions and ideas and seek out opportunities.
- ► You will not be waiting for the right or better time to go after what you want – because your time is now!

---

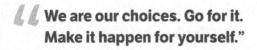 **We are our choices. Go for it.
Make it happen for yourself."**

## Coaching Questions

**1** What would be different if I played big?

**2** Is my plan brave enough?

**3** What would my future self say about my life goals?

**4** What new experiences can I create?

**5** Who do I know who has played big in the world and who will inspire me?

**6** What is truly possible if I own what I know I can do?

**7** What is truly possible if I just get started now on the project of living my bigger life?

## TP #11

# Busy is not sexy

**Beware the barrenness of a busy life.**
Socrates

I had just about finished this book when I came back and added this thought-provoker. I am an expert on being busy. I'm a single mum of three, who works full-time and travels for work, after all!

There are always so many commitments in my day: emails, phone calls, bills to pay, work to organise, clients to deliver services to, the accountant to meet, the school runs, friends to see, tradies to organise, staff to consult with, Kung Fu, exercise, shopping – and don't even ask me how many loads of washing I do in a week.

So, yes, I get being busy.

I think for many years, however, we have made 'busy' a measure of the fullness of our life and the commitment to our job and family. Busy has become the new black – a sexy, desirable thing. 'What's going on with you?'... 'Oh, I'm so busy.' 'Really? That's great. Better to be busy than bored...' blah, blah, blah. (Just quietly, I'm not sure I remember the last time I was bored. It sounds wonderful.)

The thing is, busy is often just a different version of being stressed. When we are rushing, stretched to our limit and have no time to think or relax, 'busy' negatively impacts our body. It's not sexy at all!

Busy is kind of a made up and reactive 'state', but we can more proactively tell ourselves a different story. We can choose to enjoy the busyness, the challenges and the discomfort – or we can say NO.

We can take care of ourselves, we can pace ourselves, we can delegate or get help, we can prioritise what is most important, we can let go of stuff we're not good at and don't enjoy, we can do our job differently (work smarter not harder), get a different job, organise and manage the work better, and create space for people, relaxation and fun...

The reality is that most high-performing people I have coached were never too busy for coaching; they were never too busy for things that mattered to them. Busy was not part of their vocabulary. It wasn't something they talked about.

## The bottom line on busy

The word 'busy' tells our brain to be stressed and on alert. Wipe the word from your vocabulary wherever possible.

 **Activity**

Multiply your age by 365 days – this is your current age in days.

Subtract that number from 27,375 days – that's the current average life span.

What will you miss if you are so busy being busy?

Make each day count.

# Coaching Questions

**1** Do I just need to reframe my busyness? Am I actually happy with busyness and just need to change my language to reflect that?

**2** How often do I say (moan), 'I am busy'?

**3** Do I feel my heart rate increase when I think about how busy I am?

**4** Is my sleep disturbed because I'm busy in my head?

**5** Do I feel overwhelmed by my busyness?

**6** Do I feel disempowered by my busyness, as though it's out of my control?

**7** Am I ready to make some changes around my negatively busy state of being?

**8** Am I prepared to annoy some people by pulling back, pulling out, saying no, making changes?

**9** What strategies can I put in place to create balance, space and stillness?

**10** What strategies can I put in place to manage the work?

**11** Do I know what might happen for me if I step out of busy?

*Don't say you don't have enough time. You have exactly the same number of hours per day that were given to Helen Keller, Louis Pasteur, Michelangelo, Mother Teresa, Leonardo da Vinci, Thomas Jefferson and Albert Einstein.*

**H. Jackson Brown, Jr.**

## TP #12

# Pick your battles

**Don't let something that doesn't matter take energy away from something that does.**

The stress of life provokes plenty of anger and aggression, and people can do really hurtful things. We're even inventing new terminology: think 'road rage' and 'hangry'. Anger is a normal human emotion, and it serves a purpose in readying us for a fight, flight or whatever.

However, if your default response is to fight at every provocation and you just go with that, it's exhausting! I'm not necessarily talking about fisticuffs or yelling insults and accusations or getting in someone's face. Probably more common battles involve passive-aggressive responses – that is, sneakier ways of expressing anger. Think sulking, sarcasm, withdrawing from interaction, low-level hostility, or isolating or undermining someone.

Allow me to get a little personal here: my mum had a few things on calm repeat when I was younger:

*'Would you jump off a cliff just because your friends did?'*

*'I'm the adult, please just do it.'*

*'Does this even matter?'*

*'Do you need to get involved?'*

*'What's the actual problem?'*

*'Just sleep on it and maybe it will be clearer in the morning.'*

She picked her battles (with me) and encouraged me to pick mine (with whomever). She taught me that sometimes we need to take the battle on promptly, assertively and cleverly (not aggressively), but other times if we just chill (not simmer) and go with the flow a while (calm it down), things may resolve or at least be more resolvable.

## ʃʃ Sometimes I choose peace..."

Battles drain us. If we're out there fighting all the time, we'll expend most of our energy on stuff that isn't, or shouldn't be, our priority. We'll be sitting in negativity. We'll be driven by the need to 'win' at all costs. We'll lose sight of what is actually important and what we really want.

As a parent I now say, 'Pick your battles'. As a coach, I say it to my clients when they need to define and direct where to best invest their energy. And to save my own energy, I remind myself of this constantly. (And, yes, I say the jumping off the cliff thing to my children now too!)

Pick your battles. Manage your perception of events. Step back to gain a proper perspective and choose your response, if any. Oh, and build skills to be effectively assertive if you need to be, so that you are better positioned when you do choose to take the battle on.

Choose very consciously what is worth fighting for and how you want to 'be' and live your life. You will never get today again – so clear your mind, calm your body, and pick your battles. (I also say to my children: 'Sometimes it's better to be kind than right.')

## The bottom line on battles

Please don't interpret this as permission to step away from a responsibility that is yours. This is not about being passive or apathetic; rather, it is about knowing what is important and worth standing up for, and about being able to look back and be proud of you – how you handled yourself and others. This is about emotionally intelligent living, and not wasting energy on things that you can justifiably let go of and things you don't actually have control over. A good test is to consider whether the battle will really matter to you in a year's time. Know what you stand for, use your values as a compass for decision-making and be consistent in your choices.

Have you noticed that there are people who consistently attract drama? Or who sit in victimhood, gathering support against the 'enemy'? It's often because they draw energy from negativity. You will not see me fighting for something that isn't absolutely aligned with how I want to live my life, or spending any more time than I have to with people who spread negativity. Take care of you; remember you are your most important project.

# Coaching Questions

1. Are there battles going on in my life that are not worth my time and energy?

2. What battles could/should I step out of?

3. What would happen if I just let this (or that) battle go?

4. What battle(s) should I take on?

5. How much does this really matter to me and my future and my wellbeing?

6. Do I need to win this? What are the benefits of fighting this battle?

7. What is the cost if I go into battle over this?

8. What skills or behaviours do I need to learn more about to effectively manage myself 'in battle'?

9. Am I serving the future version of me – picking my battles and 'fighting' the good fight in ways that when I look back, I can be proud of myself?

## TP #13
# An Italian affair

**Sometimes I feel like an Italian who is trapped in an Australian body.**

Yes, I want you to feel envious and ooh and ahh as you read this! Not really. But this is the coolest thing I have ever done, if it's possible to be cool in your forties! What I really want here is for you to feel inspired. To take on board what you hear all the time – that we are all capable of more than we imagine, and if you dream it you can do it, so go make it happen. Go after what you really want. Mostly, you won't regret the things you do in life. It's much more likely you'll regret the things you don't do.

So here's my story: I took my three children out of school for an entire term and we went and lived in Italy. We took Italian lessons before we left and then immersed ourselves for three months in everything Italian. We ate pizza and gelati every day. We slept in late and didn't have dinner until 10 pm most nights. I woke up with my children every day for three months, which was the greatest blessing – given my 'normal' life requires me to travel and be away.

We missed trains, got lost and felt earthquakes. We sat on top of the leaning tower of Pisa, and on a different day we pretended we could hear the tigers in the Colosseum. We went on the 'canoes' (as Mabel called the gondolas) in Venice. We caught the chair lift to the top of Capri and went ice-skating outside at 11 pm in Lake Como. We avoided riots in Florence and laughed at the waiters serving my 15-year-old wine in Tuscany. We ate dinner in castles and had conversations based on hand gestures with locals. Watching the Italian ladies hand-making pasta is joyful and the colours of the Cinque Terre find me in my dreams.

I should be clear here that there was no romantic Italian affair with a man named Giovanni. Let's remember I was travelling with three children. There was a man in Lake Como who sent a drink to my table, and a few moments later was joined by his wife. I know – outrageous! – and also a fun story to tell.

This chapter in my story was defining, though. It was me saying f**k off to the universe. Despite the challenges that had been thrown my way, I was going to find a way to be a life-lover. It's incredible, isn't it, to know that we can go from self-medicating with wine in the foetal position, to amazing adventures all in one lifetime? I draw on my Italian memories on a daily basis. My children and I live off the stories and have nearly forgotten all the bad bits.

It's interesting to me that people regularly respond to this story by saying, 'I would never be able to do that!' The reality is, the trip did take planning. I had to ensure my business could run without me on a daily basis, and lots of other things. But here's what's amazing; it didn't cost as much as you might think. We stayed in Airbnbs, we caught trains, pizza is cheap and there were nights of cheese on fresh bread with a tomato and basil salad. It costs little to walk and sightsee all day.

We just decided that we would go, that we would find a way, that we would trust that our friends and family would be well and happy while we were away, and that my business would keep ticking over. Once the big decision was made, the detail started falling into place.

People did think I was crazy to go travelling with three children on my own. And you know what? It did feel a little crazy and even irresponsible, but brave and ever so exciting as well. My children learned so much about travel and being organised and taking responsibility and staying safe and another culture.

The experience and time together was more precious than I can say. This type of experience does change you. Apart from the fact that both my boys took up drinking coffee, we have an entirely new way of thinking about the world and our relationships with people.

I came back from Italy with an even greater appreciation of my children, red wine, siesta and peace.

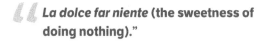 **La dolce far niente (the sweetness of doing nothing)."**

Do it! Live the life you dream of. Create the life you want, one step at a time. Start with the essentials in life: first you need to be safe, warm, fed and clothed and have somewhere to sleep. Then you need to invest in relationships, to love and be loved, and feel good about yourself; you need to get healthy, find a job you enjoy, save some money. Then you're ready to fly! But, hey, feel free to jump straight to fly if you like.

# Coaching Questions

**1** What dreams do I have that could become a reality if I just made the decision to do/to go/to start?

**2** Is my home my happy place, my place of sanctuary and peace that recharges me? If not, what do I need to change?

**3** Do my relationships nurture and support me and add to the quality of my life? If not, what do I need to change?

**4** Do I have the 'infrastructure' to support living my dreams – for example, savings, insurance, positive supporters?

**5** What experiences will enrich my life? (Start small and work your way up: more cuddles, a new hobby or project, lunch in the park, volunteer work, an ice-cream on the jetty, a walk in a gallery, some study, more time with loved ones and friends, more friends...)

**6** What makes me laugh out loud, and how can I get more of that?

**7** What makes me feel alive and full of energy, and how can I get more of that?

**8** How can I be brave and stretch myself, get out of my comfort zone, and do new things and have new thoughts?

**9** What's my version of 'an Italian affair', and how can I achieve that?

**10** What are the greatest 'gifts' I could give myself? When I'm 80, what will my best memories be?

## TP #14
# My job is what I do, not who I am

**People will value who I am the most, not what I do.**

Please don't judge me harshly as I confess to having watched every single episode of *Sex and the City*. I swear Carrie has plenty to teach us all, men and women, young and old. There's an episode in 'An American Girl in Paris' where Miranda asks Carrie, 'How could you quit your job? It's who you are.' And Carrie replies, 'No, it's not who I am; it's what I do!' I remember hearing this and storing it as something I always wanted to remember.

In my work in the corporate world and especially in coaching people, I come across many who are high-flying success stories. But I also come across many who are in crisis, who have lost jobs, wealth, partners or status – and, along with that, their sense of self and wellbeing and direction. They are floundering and trying to find their way back to success, in their job and, therefore, in life.

The workplace (and life) can be tough. It can gobble up the best of people and spit them out! They're left to pick themselves up, dust themselves off and somehow get back in the ring.

If we define ourselves and find our self-worth in narrow dimensions – for example, through just our current role, work or achievements – we become vulnerable and super-sensitive to failure. And we can lose sight of what is most important to us. We lose perspective. We can accidently devalue the core of ourselves, our central being, the most important part of who we are and what drives and fulfils us. We can also accidently devalue what matters most – our relationships and our quality of life.

## The bottom line on finding perspective

- As a coach, I encourage people to look at their lives more holistically and to look for who they uniquely are – where they've been and what they've learned so far and where they want to go (looking into their future).
- I ask them to think about what brings them joy, what fulfils them, what is most meaningful to them and what they really want from life.
- I encourage people to find perspective on success at work; it's only one aspect of their life, and often not the most important aspect of their life – even though it may feel that way.

I am a mum, friend, daughter, cousin, mentor, coach, speech-maker, traveller of the world and so much more. In our lifetime we spend so many hours working, so it's kind of important that we have purposeful work or a career that is enriching. But we are so much more than just what we do.

I am not my education. I am not my body. I am not my job. I am not my bank account. I am not my family. I am not my past. I am not my future.

I am a whole person. My full potential is not yet known. I have dreams I haven't thought of yet. And there are people coming into my world who might alter its course. The exciting part is that it's not all mapped out yet.

If we do not define ourselves just by our job, but rather find self-worth across the broader spectrum of life's activities, we can more easily manage the hard bits in our working life. We have a broader base, a greater resilience and more ways to find fulfillment and happiness. We can more easily put ourselves in charge of ourselves.

 **Don't ask me what I do; ask me who I am."**

# Coaching Questions

**1** Does what's happening at work, negatively affect every other area of my life?

**2** Am I too regularly giving the best of me to my work?

**3** Do I have a proper balance – time for relaxation, play, family and friends, as well as work?

**4** Do I have a successful alignment between my working and personal lives, where each gives me energy and resources for the other, and each gives way to the other only as truly necessary?

**5** How much more successful would I be in my career if other parts of my life were in good order?

**6** How much more fulfilled would I be in my life if work was not draining me?

**7** Do I depend on my results and relationships at work for happiness?

**8** How else do I measure success and/or happiness?

**9** Where are the gaps for me? What needs to be a higher priority – for example, health, personal relationships, spirituality, living circumstances, recreational activities, giving to my community, ongoing learning and stimulation...?

**10** Do I know who I am – my strengths and weaknesses, passions and pleasures, drivers and dreams? And am I clear about what I truly want from my life?

# Watch what people do, rather than what they say

**Your behaviour and choices tell me everything I need to know about you.**

Think about all the times people annoyed, angered, harassed, frustrated, hurt or confused you! We could all write books about the dysfunctional ways adults sometimes interact with one another.

Here is something I know for sure: most communication is non-verbal. People do not always tell their truth, but they do always show us what they are thinking and feeling, and what they are about. If we concentrate on 'seeing' and understanding them rather than just listening to their words, we will understand them far better.

So pay less attention to the words others use. Rather, get up close and personal, ask lots of questions, listen really well, and pay most attention to their behaviour and body language. Look at their current behaviour and also think about their past behaviour. Listen more than talk. Seek first to understand and then to be understood.

Think about the people you admire and respect who are good people and good communicators. It's likely they consistently behave in a way that you understand and trust. Their body language matches their words and, most especially, they are authentic and true to themselves. They don't play games. They don't work to hidden agendas. They are genuinely interested in people. They are good and kind. They inspire confidences and trust.

I'm a secret geek when it comes to understanding why people behave the way they do.

## The bottom line on behaviour

- ► People behave in a way that works for them.
- ► People treat us the way we let them treat us.

### tip

If you find yourself getting hurt, ignored, overpowered (or whatever) in your conversations, pay more attention to the other person's behaviour. Once you understand what is truly driving them, you can better manage them and yourself within the conversation.

Learn to manage your own body language so you are sending the signals you mean. For instance, if you want to show confidence, prepare yourself and what you have to say. Stand/ sit tall, uncross your arms, speak clearly and concisely, look the person in the eye and manage what your face is doing. Remember you often get back what you give out.

If you are strategically building, defining or evolving your personal 'brand', consider how others would describe how you behave. My experience tells me that behaving with integrity and authenticity is what people are attracted to.

# Coaching Questions

1. What behaviours do I observe but ignore?

2. How can I be more alert to what people are doing around me and to me?

3. What would be different if I paid specific attention to people's behaviour?

4. Are there some people in my life who take advantage of me?

5. How would others describe my behaviour?

6. Do I do what I say I am going to do? (This is the most basic definition of trustworthiness.)

## TP #16
# Curiosity always

**Only the curious have something to find, something to learn, something more to be. I have no special talents. I am only passionately curious.**

**Albert Einstein**

Now I don't want to sound overly dramatic, but when I very suddenly became a single mum, valuing curiosity was a really beneficial trait.

There's a very big difference between 'OMG, how will I cope as a single mother?' and 'What will I now need to do/learn?' And between 'How on earth will I survive financially?' and 'What new activities/opportunities will I need to pursue?'

I don't want it to sound as if I found all the answers – curiosity won't always work. Positivity won't always kick in. Sometimes a tantrum is needed – to vent! And sometimes crying on the floor in the foetal position is a great way to get it all out there and give yourself a hug. I became, for a while, highly competent at both these responses! But when I had vented and cried and was ready to move back into adult mode, I started self-coaching and became curious about my way forward.

Curiosity involves asking better questions, exploring with an open mind and being inquisitive at every opportunity.

Children are so great at this. They don't assume they already know everything, they don't have to be right and they don't let ego drive their learning. They can meander through a situation, looking at this and that, spending unhurried time thinking about whatever comes to mind and wondering what else might be around. They don't worry about failure. They don't feel constrained by how things have been before. They look at things bright-eyed, openly, freshly, optimistically – they're curious about all the possibilities.

I'm a bit of an expert on curiosity, actually. My company name is Curious Consulting Pty Ltd. What I love most about curiosity is that it creates freedom and removes layers of judgment and constraint. Getting curious is actually quite fun!

There is intellectual curiosity (what more is there to know) and emotional curiosity (what more is there for me).

## The bottom line on curiosity

- ➤ I invite you to think about what getting more curious would mean for you across all aspects of your life.
- ➤ Intellectually, what can you ask, think, learn or research?
- ➤ Emotionally, what can be different or better in your life? Could you build better relationships with others if you spent more time investing in understanding how they feel about whatever is happening?

# Coaching Questions

**1** What would be different if I were curious instead of upset?

**2** What would be different if I asked questions rather than made statements?

**3** How would I feel if I imagined new possibilities?

**4** What do I wonder about that I need to do something about?

**5** What ideas might come if I were more open and childlike in my thinking?

**6** Am I known for being great at asking questions? If not, am I ready to instil this as a new behaviour?

**7** How would my relationships change if I were known for valuing a curious approach? What would happen if I became more interested in the point of view of others?

## TP #17

# The rockstar version of you

As a rockstar I have two instincts: to have fun and change the world. I have a chance to do both.
Bono

If life were easy and all our dreams came true, we would all be amazingly successful over-achievers: famous, rich, smart, talented, successful, attractive, super-athletes, perfect parents.

But life's not like that and that would be boring anyway, wouldn't it?

I want you to take a moment to remember back to when you were a child and all things were possible: being a rockstar, garbage collector, ballerina, astronaut, model or explorer were all totally realistic career options.

But to make my point here, I'm going for rockstar. Think Pink, Beyonce, Prince (bless him), or whoever rocks your boat. I'm going to put before you what it takes to be a rockstar, with the emphasis on the star part.

Let's look at what rockstars have done to get to where they are. Firstly, they do something well – they hone their skills and they practise and practise. They pick their genre and refine their 'act'; they know how they want to present themselves and what they want to be known for. They learn as much as they can about their specialty area. They learn from others, from books, from trial and error – however they can. They work and work, and every time they get knocked down, they get back up and try again. They're determined, they're focused on their goal, they believe in themselves and they persevere.

They know it won't be easy and they know it's up to them to make success happen. They get disillusioned sometimes, but they just keep going. They're passionate about what they're doing, and they have fun and probably shed a few tears along the way.

They do everything possible to make it. They commit to punishing touring schedules and know they might have to start small and work their way up. They know that every person they meet is a potential fan, and that every time they go on stage it is an opportunity. They are working to be the very best version of themselves every single time they record or perform.

They continue to grow, improve, learn, create and evolve. They put themselves out there at every opportunity: gigs, interviews, press conferences, media releases and social media. They let people see who they really, uniquely are.

Some, looking for energy, longevity, good looks and good feelings – think Pink, Sting, Mick Jagger – also commit fully to looking after themselves.

OK, you get the idea I hope. But here's what I want to say. Many rockstars look pretty ordinary in their Grade Six school photos, and they come from pretty ordinary backgrounds – quite possibly just like me and you. But what got them rockstar status was their drive and commitment to their goal. And we can all do that, be our own version of a rockstar.

We just need to do... well, all of the above. Find our passion and be the best version of ourselves.

So how am I being the very best version of me? (Thank you for asking.) Well, I plan my food, I schedule exercise, I educate myself and I take on career opportunities that are terrifying. I persevere.

Change and challenge and big goals are hard and uncomfortable. And things don't always go to plan; life throws us curve balls and sometimes we fumble or even drop them!

But the rockstar version of you is so full of possibility, fun and adventure. This is where dreams live. When we are rockstars in our own world, magic happens. We become obsessed, consumed and passionate. Everything is different when we have the vision and we're prepared to do the work and go after what we want.

Who did you want to be, before you became a grown up? And/or (think big here), who or what do you really want to be now?

**Take action. Start now – take a first small step towards getting closer to who or what you want to be.**

## Coaching Questions

1. Do I know who my inner rockstar is?

2. Does it matter to me if I don't live the dream?

3. What skills and knowledge do I have that serve me in going after my rockstar dream?

4. Who do I know who could mentor me?

5. Am I having enough fun in my life?

6. Do I remember what I am passionate about?

7. Am I prepared to do what's required?

8. What are the consequences of me doing nothing?

9. How do I get started?

## TP #18
# Truth tellers

**When someone tells us the truth, it is equal to growth and opportunity. Why wouldn't we intentionally seek that out?**

Surround yourself with people who tell you the truth! Well, at least find two or three of them. It might be a friend, mentor or a coach. It might be someone you pay (a coach) or a lifelong friend.

Many clients I've coached have an entire cheer squad of people who support, encourage and challenge them. Of course, YOU have a major responsibility here. No one wants to tell you the truth if they think they are risking the relationship and they believe you are going to hold it against them.

So how are you with feedback? Do you value a different perspective? Do you accept that others often see you differently from how you see yourself?

If you give people permission to tell you the truth about what they are observing in you, you have a chance to examine all the information about who you are being, rather than just half of it – your own perspective. This process recognises that communication is a two-way thing; it's about not just the 'face' you choose to show people, but also their perception of you.

It doesn't mean their different perception is the 'truth' about you, or that you have to agree with them or adapt for them.

But when we hear someone else's viewpoint, we become more acutely self-aware and more knowledgeable about the impact we can have on others. We have the chance to reflect, change, improve and grow.

This is also about taking responsibility for our words and actions. When we know we are going to be accountable to another person, that we will be receiving feedback, we are more mindful of the choices we make.

Part of why clients come to see me as a coach is because I ask them not simply 'why?' or 'what happened?' Rather, I ask 'What else was/is possible?' One of my favourites is when clients say to me, 'I don't know what to do', and I get to say, 'Well, what would you do if you did know?' Or I might ask, 'What would a person you admire do?'

Feedback is not just about people telling you 'the truth', but also about inviting you to create more, and perhaps better, possibilities and opportunities for yourself in how you are working and living.

tip

**Be intentional about this thought-provoker. Set up times to meet with your truth tellers. Get them all together and see what happens – I dare you!**

**They'll all have different perspectives. This will keep your ego in check and get/keep momentum happening. Truth tellers are the greatest gift for successful people. It's rare to make it on your own. Get on it.**

# Coaching Questions

1. Who are my truth tellers now?

2. Have I given them explicit permission?

3. Can I do the same for them?

4. Have I opened my mind to feedback I've already received?

5. Have I been paying attention to the feedback I've been receiving and changed something as a result?

6. Am I brave enough and grounded enough to really hear what people will tell me?

7. Is there someone I should approach to mentor or coach me?

8. Would it be beneficial to hire a coach?

**Keep calm and let them tell you the truth."**

## TP #19
# Celebrate

**The more you celebrate your life, the more there is in life to celebrate.**
Oprah Winfrey

Forgive me for generalising, but as adults we aren't so great at owning our success. I have noticed, however, that successful, happy and emotionally aware people *do* celebrate. They acknowledge their own success as well as the achievements of others. Often you will hear great leaders talk about how they love to create success through others. But they also celebrate their own milestones; it may be publicly or privately, and it might be a party or a gift to themselves like a holiday. The main thing is they acknowledge achievement.

I think one of the reasons many people do not celebrate success is because they focus on what they aren't doing well. And all of us have stuff we don't do well. (Ask my team how I am with reading reports or talking technology! And let's just say, trying to teach me even basic accounting will be like hitting your head against a brick wall!)

Apologies in advance to all the HR people and team leaders out there, but many of them spend too many hours discussing knowledge gaps, identifying opportunities for growth and writing development plans – and too little time acknowledging success.

The result of many training dollars is well-developed weaknesses, and people painfully getting a bit better at what they're not good at and don't want to do.

I say life's short – concentrate on what you're good at and what you enjoy because that way's more fun! In individual and team coaching sessions, I always start with strengths. Imagine if we spent as much time on what we are awesome at as we do on what we could improve?

**Be awesome, and acknowledge when you are. Be your own number one fan, and make sure you're in the right job, with the right manager, where as much as possible you are doing what you're already good at. Then celebrate – everything!**

**Celebrating can be quietly done if that is your nature. Successful people have healthy self-talk so, at the very least, have a chat with yourself and give yourself a pat on the back. Be proud of you.**

 **Activity**

I encourage all my coaching clients to keep a journal for at least three months. Try this out. Every night write out:

1. What did I do well today?
2. What should I have done better today?
3. What is my intention for tomorrow?

## Coaching Questions

1. Can I write down what I am most proud of over the last 12 months?

2. How do I communicate my successes with others?

3. Privately, what can I do to ensure I am acknowledging and building on my strengths?

4. What do I do to celebrate the achievements of others?

5. Am I comfortable with the story of who I am (the stuff I wish I had done differently and the moments when I have smashed it)?

# No one is coming!

**If you do not change direction, you may end up where you are heading.**
Lao Tzu

For most of us in developed nations, we have never had access to more information and learning opportunities than we have right now. We have pretty much everything we need to thrive and succeed at our fingertips.

We can find our life partners online, order dinner via our mobiles, and email our children's teachers at 1 am! We can go to gyms 24/7, order our heart's desire online, and hire-a-hubby! We can study at home, talk to a professional about any problem and travel anywhere we want.

Yet what do we have? We have significant mental health issues, an obesity crisis, sexting, bullying, loneliness, violence, corruption, poverty, unemployment, nuclear threats...

These are all BIG issues that may or may not be affecting your life. I just want to say here... there is probably no one coming to fix your life. There is no solution online and no particular organisation that will provide everything you need for a balanced, healthy, happy and successful life.

The most likely scenario is that you will need to do the work and create the change that you need. You. Yes, you!!

Access everything and everyone you can to be the best possible version of you, but don't wait for the right time and don't depend solely on an expert, a network or a single strategy. Trust you already have what you need right now to start the work on you.

It makes sense to utilise as many useful resources as you can find but, in my experience as a coach, people who are living a life they love are doing so because they made it happen themselves. They drive it and create it.

Invest your energy in you. There's something so incredibly empowering about designing your own life. Go back to thought-provoker 1 and think about your plan. There really is only one you in the world. You are the only person who has lived your life. You know you best.

**tip**

**Look back over and add to your notes. Start tidying up and refining your plan. These thought-provokers will also have added to the depth of your 'I am...' statement.**

*You have everything you need, my friend, but it will take everything you've got.*

**Barbara Nicholson, a very wise friend of mine**

# Part II Summary Coaching Questions

1. Have I got my plan together?
2. Do I know the story of me so far?
3. Am I clear about my values and the beliefs that will serve me?
4. Am I going to work as if I am my most important project?
5. Am I prepared to do what's required?
6. What am I going to unlearn?
7. Am I committed?
8. Will I proceed, trusting the future version of me?
9. Will I consciously choose what I say yes and no to?
10. Will I look for opportunities to grow my resilience?
11. Am I going to play big in the world?
12. Will I stop with busyness?
13. How will I pick my battles?
14. What's my version of 'an Italian affair'?
15. How will I be more than my job?
16. Will I proactively manage my attitude, skills and knowledge?
17. How will I value curiosity in my thinking and decision-making?
18. Do I have clarity on what my new normal will look like?

19  Will I value and listen to my truth tellers?

20  How will I celebrate myself?

21  Am I going to trust that I don't need anyone else to come and fix me?

22  If I do need help and support, what is my plan to get it?

# Part III
## Strategies for a successful life

Do you know how best to set yourself up for success? Whatever your goals, dreams or ambitions, one thing is certain; achieving them will not happen incidentally, automatically or effortlessly. I'm pretty sure you've already guessed this after working your way through the book thus far.

The strategies in this part of *Read Me First* will not only accelerate your success, but also support your evolution in a way that is sustainable. In 20 years of coaching, I have found that these are the things that consistently work.

You've already had a lot to think about, but these 15 strategies will change the way you think, behave and feel, and lead you towards a more successful life (whatever that looks like for you):

1. Change your mind
2. Pay attention
3. Own your regrets
4. Find your tribe
5. Live like a city
6. Intention
7. Don't go along to get along
8. People can suck!
9. Head and heart
10. Know your super powers
11. The verandah test
12. Baby steps, big jumps
13. Solution-focused thinking
14. Play
15. The reality check

# Change your mind

**Whether you think you can or think you can't, you're right...**
Henry Ford

In the normal course of things, by adulthood our brain pathways are becoming a bit more 'hard-wired'. We become habituated to, and protective of, how things 'are', and we subconsciously look for evidence that all we've already learned is true and enough.

This is a normal, survival kind of thing.

I'm here to tell you that this dynamic, normal though it may be, does not serve you well in terms of achieving your higher goals.

In my work as a success coach, I'm frequently calling on clients to change their mind, flex their thinking and adapt their behaviour.

When coaching I will often ask:

*'What's a different way you could think about that?'*

Please take on board that what you're thinking directly affects how you're feeling – so start there when you want to make positive changes.

If you want to be an emotionally intelligent 'grown-up', become more conscious of what you're thinking and be ready to change that thinking.

The awareness of the impact of your thinking is the first step in changing your mind (and your life). The critical bit is in the second step, which is your ability to reframe your own thinking, to move on from what you might have thought before and decide anew what meaning you will give an event, experience, situation or feeling.

### ✎ Activity

How will I consciously change and manage my own thinking and beliefs so that I evolve and grow?

_____

_____

_____

_____

_____

_____

_____

_____

_____

_____

## Strategy #2
# Pay attention

**We become what we pay attention to.**

Pay attention – to everything!

We are sensory beings, constantly receiving messages from our environment and the people around us, mentally, emotionally, physically and socially.

But are you listening?

Are you getting enough stimulation, nutrition, exercise and sleep?

Are your relationships healthy and fulfilling?

When did you last feel joy and lightness?

Are you thinking good thoughts?

Are you being kind to you and others? Are you solving your problems or getting stuck on them?

You can't control other people; the smart thing is to pay more attention to your own self-talk. What stories have you been repeating over and over? What do you need to let go of and change? Who or what needs to be left behind? There are things you already know you should be doing differently: take notice of those voices in your head, that feeling in your gut and the messages from your body. When we don't pay attention, the universe often slaps us!

**Activity**

If you want more peace and less frustration, take some time to reflect on what you have been ignoring and make notes below. Move out of apathy and proactively make better decisions, implement changes and act. There will never be a better time than right now. (Don't wait for Monday!)

How will you keep focused on the areas of your life that are calling out for your attention?

_____

_____

_____

_____

_____

_____

_____

_____

_____

_____

# Own your regrets

**It will not be easy, but it will be worth it...**

OMG! Have them! We associate the word 'regrets' with such negativity but I don't want a life without them.

Carrying guilt for your regrets, however, is corrosive. We should learn from our past, but let's not live there.

My package of regrets encompasses all the things I've done or not done that I feel sad, repentant or disappointed about. But how would I learn and grow from my experiences if I hadn't had them?

A life well and fully lived will be full of regrets: failures, missteps, errors of judgment and actions not taken.

If you want to be someone who evolves and grows, and if you want stories to reflect on and wisdom that you can benefit from and share, then I say go for it – without fear of failure or regret!

When I'm old and grey I want a long list of regrets – and may that list make me laugh and cry and stir many fine memories.

Regrets are part of the deal if you want a life that is lived across its full spectrum, full of light and shade and colour.

Successful people don't get it right all the time; I can tell you this for sure. Anyone who has achieved something they are proud of has messed up majorly.

If you're waiting to feel good enough and smart enough, the time may never come.

## Activity

May your biggest regrets serve your future happiness. So live your life fully. Get on the roller-coaster. Be brave. Put yourself out there. Bring it on!

How will you do this? Write some ideas down here.

List the regrets that you hold and reframe them into a learning lesson here.

_____

_____

_____

_____

_____

_____

_____

_____

_____

## Strategy #4
# Find your tribe

**Surround yourself with people who want you to succeed, who will challenge you to be more and will make you laugh...**

#yourtribe

Surround yourself with people who enrich your life.

You'll have your besties (hopefully), who have got you more closely covered, who will pick you up off the shower floor on your worst day, who trust you and are trustworthy, who believe in you and back you.

However, I have always believed that a handful of people can't be expected to give me everything I need and want.

Your larger tribe are the people who collectively make life better, funnier, fuller, more interesting, active and rewarding.

They are the ones who are in life with you and care about what matters to you. They stretch and challenge you.

They make you think more deeply and more broadly.

They push you to be a better person. Your tribe lives your dreams alongside you.

They make you laugh, sweat and do things you wouldn't do on your own.

They don't have to know each other but they do need to do or be something that adds to your life. (Your tribe might have your new best friend in it.)

Your tribe extends out beyond family and best friends to include your community, your workplace, your network and your world. There are no energy vampires in your tribe.

Motivational speaker Jim Rohn wisely said, 'We are the average of the five people that we spend the most time with.'

We are all meant to have a sense of belonging in the world and to contribute to it. It's all about the people you choose to hang out with.

 **Activity**

Cultivate friends. Be interested in, and care for, your tribe. And let them care about you! How will you do this?

Write out the names of people who are already in your tribe. Then review your list and see if there are any who will not serve the future version of you. Also identify people who you would love in your tribe but don't know yet – for example, mentors, experts…

_____

_____

_____

_____

_____

_____

_____

_____

## Strategy #5
# Live like a city

**Work like New York and eat like Italy.**

I am always fascinated by how different cities in the world make me feel.

Travel broadens my horizons and gives me more options for how I live my life.

In London I'm into theatre.

In Sorrento (Italy) I sleep in and meditate.

In San Francisco I tap into my inner hippy and ride a bike!

I lead my consulting business as though I'm in New York – we go hard, respond fast and our clients think we don't sleep!

Even if you can't be travelling the world, the message is to deliberately seek out ways to experience different environments, people and places.

Enrich and broaden your life. Learn from anybody and everybody. Think bigger. Believe you can have, and deserve to have, a great life. Otherwise, how will you know when you are at your best and happiest?

This is about self-care, self-belief and success (whatever your version of success is).

Whoever you are, whether you're reading this as a middle-aged man or a single mum, think: what kind of environment brings me high energy and inspiration?

Your places might not be London or New York, but rather a restaurant, sanctuary in your garden, riverside campsite, art gallery or that shiny corner office you want to step into.

### ✎ Activity

Make decisions from a place where you are at your best. Where do you need to be?

Where are you and what are you doing when you are in flow and living to your potential? Which city would you be?

_____

_____

_____

_____

_____

_____

_____

## Strategy #6
# Intention

**Our intention is directly connected to how we feel and what we have achieved.**

One strategy I suggest to my coaching clients is to be very specific about how you fill your day.

If you want to move forward to greater success, each night write down what you did well that day (celebrate), what you could have done better (development) and what matters for you tomorrow (intention).

When you rise each day, aim to be clear about who you are going to be in the world and what you need to do to move a step closer to a happy and successful you.

Having *attention* means you have awareness of what you want, where you are going and how you will get there.

Having *intention* is the accountability system; the plan you have in place to get what you want.

For example, if you want to get physically fit, you might get a personal trainer. Or if you want to get life fit, you will have reviewed who you have been and who you want to be, and you will have a plan to get from one to the other.

If today you have made a decision (commitment) to be a kinder person, tonight you will reflect on how well you did that and what you need to do better tomorrow.

Your attention informs your intention, which is supported by your plan.

Your intention is what you come back to at the end of each day.

### ✎ Activity

I know, goals and strategies – blah, blah, blah. But I need to tell you, there's a reason every self-help guru in the world will tell you to write down your goals and have a plan with specific strategies (it's because it works!).

Write down your intentions here.

*My intention for tomorrow is...* _____

_____

_____


*My intention for this month is...* _____

_____

_____

_____


*When I get to the end of this year, I will have...* _____

_____

_____

_____

_____

_____

_____

## Strategy #7
# Don't go along to get along

**Step forward and step up...**

We all know people who go through the motions but lack independent thought. We're all guilty of that sometimes.

It's easier than having to be awesome every day! How exhausting would that be? Sometimes we just want to sleep and watch Netflix.

Everywhere you look, you will see people who are settling. They have OK jobs and satisfactory lives.

However, I'm here to say loud and clear:

*'Don't do that!'*

Don't be the sheep following the flock.

Don't be the teddy bear, trying to please everyone.

If you want to create something amazing in your life, you need to step into YOUR potential.

Be robust in your thinking and challenge yourself each day. When you put your head on the pillow each night you need to know that you did something courageous or tried something new.

Step out of busy and into conscious choices.

I often get calls from people who wake up one day and realise that five years have passed since they decided they wanted something different, since they decided to do something. In what feels like a minute, they're just... older! And not necessarily wiser or better off.

## Activity

Now that you've read this, you won't let that happen, right? Don't just go along to get along. Get going on your own path and take the first step now, today! What is that first step for you?

Identify any areas of your life where you have been going along to get along. Make notes here. Perhaps it's in your career or in a relationship.

_____

_____

_____

_____

_____

_____

_____

_____

_____

_____

## Strategy #8
# People can suck!

**Not everyone will love you but love them anyway.
Not everyone is fair but play fair anyway. Not everyone
will tell you the truth, but be honest anyway.**
Me, kind of

Be prepared to be hurt, to be lied to and to be treated poorly, unfairly and harshly at times.

Expect the worst as well as the best of people, because unbeknown to you, people are going through their own drama, stress, grief, anger, tiredness and frustration.

Many are poor communicators, they haven't grown up well-loved and with good role models, and they are scarred by their negative experiences.

Some are ill, on medication with side-effects, not sleeping because of a newborn, grieving, divorcing, starving themselves, unable to have children, going bankrupt, subject to domestic violence, drug-addicted, failing, unhappy. Some are overly ambitious, egocentric, narcissistic, power-hungry, just awful or bad!

People let you down sometimes.

They might be jealous of your success, and sabotage or undermine you and talk negatively about you. Some people may just not like you and some are just different from you.

Adults often have an agenda and are super competent at manipulating to get what they need; people generally behave in a way that gets them the results they are after.

There is great news, though. You can believe and trust that there is much good out there, and that the very best of everything is still there for you.

You are going to meet people who will inspire you, and you will surprise yourself with what you can do when you are really tested.

You do not need to give people the power to derail you and bring you down. In my experience, the things that people do that annoy us are often the traits we least like about ourselves.

I have met people who have inspired me so much that they made my heart hurt. I get excited about who I will sit next to on a plane. People are fascinating and surprising. Roll with all of them. There are so many perfect moments in the everyday and more incredible people are coming your way!

## Activity

It's your job to look after you. What strategies will you use to protect your energy, plan and heart?

_____

_____

_____

_____

_____

_____

## Strategy #9
# Head and heart

**What you know in your head and what you feel in your heart matters equally.**

In my work as a coach I have spent thousands of hours listening... Listening to people work through how they will make decisions, create change and live their lives.

Most people naturally lean towards one of two tendencies. They are either:

- a feeler (and I don't mean in a weird way); or
- a thinker.

I listen to the thinker as he/she tells me their logic, reasons and evidence for their current thinking. Then I will ask them to put that to the side for a moment and I'll ask them questions they hadn't yet thought of.

These questions will require that they think more deeply, more broadly, more strategically, more holistically – and in a more heartfelt and personal way.

If you are naturally someone who feels and goes with intuition, take time to also be practical and apply logic.

For you to really honour who you are, I am suggesting you process everything that is in your head and also consider where your heart sits.

If you are someone who thinks deeply, analyses everything and maybe even overthinks things, take time to get in touch with your feelings. This is not a fluffy coaching idea. This more holistic and balanced approach gets results.

And an ability to do this with others will absolutely create more respectful relationships.

Listen to your head AND heart!

 **Activity**

Think of a recent decision you made with your heart or with your head. How could you have done that differently? If it was a decision made with your heart, what logic or further thought could you have given to it? If the decision was made purely with your head, what would have been different if you had considered it from a more personal or emotive perspective?

Make your notes here and don't underestimate the power of this strategy.

_____

_____

_____

_____

_____

_____

_____

_____

_____

_____

## Strategy #10
# Know your super powers

**You are good at lots of things. Tell me what you are extraordinary at! That is your super power.**

Get on it! Be optimistic and immodest here. Blow your own trumpet, know your brand, perfect your elevator pitch!

Successful people know what their strengths are and what drives them, and they can talk about it without sounding arrogant.

I know that time travel, an ability to walk through walls and super human strength could be fun, but let's get serious about your actual super powers.

People who create a career and life based on their super powers smash it!

So how do you know what they are? Think about what you do that has (or could have) real impact. (Hopefully it's impactful in a good way, not an evil way!)

What are you really good at and what do you really enjoy? (These are often the same thing.) If you walk into an interview with me, this is one of the very first questions I will ask you.

For example, if you have an ability to connect with people from all walks of life, consider how you can maximise that. If you're really good at information technology, do that. If you are really interested in a particular thing, study it.

Ask others what they think your super powers might be.

Super powers are behavioural attributes.

### ✎ Activity

Make a list of the behaviours you demonstrate daily that show people who you are. Then pick the one that serves you most to become the best version of you.

I love to ask people to outline their super powers in an interview. Be really specific here. This might make the difference between someone saying yes instead of no to you.

_____

_____

_____

_____

_____

_____

_____

_____

_____

_____

_____

_____

## Strategy #11
# The verandah test

**Your life will be a reflection of the decisions you are making now.**

My friend and mentor, David Hornery, taught me this. He said to ask myself this question on a regular basis: When I'm 80 and sitting on the verandah, what do I want to be able to remember, say, think, do and feel?

- What will be my best memories, best stories and finest achievements?

- What will have made me happy and unhappy?

- What will I be proud of and ashamed of? What are the standout big moments, big problems and big successes?

And, importantly, of all the millions of things I worried about, stressed over and felt unhappy about, what actually mattered in the end?

There's such a freedom in overlaying this thinking and asking these questions in everyday life: if I do this and fail, will I care when I'm on the verandah?

What would the 80-year-old me advise me to do here?

When I'm on the verandah, will I even remember this thing that seems overwhelming right now?

Will it matter then that my child shaved his head? Will this thing that seems a disaster now be just a funny story later?

Will my 80-year-old self wish I'd picked this path rather than that one? Or behaved this way rather than that way? Or put more effort in here or there?

This is about maintaining proper perspective, having a balanced view, and living to your higher priorities and your values. And dare I borrow the phrase, 'not sweating the small stuff'? This is about keeping your eye on the bigger picture and the longer term.

Successful people are awesome at working out where to invest their energy. They don't worry about things that won't matter later. They take risks that allow them to grow, and they forgive themselves in advance for the choices that didn't work out.

*(By the way, I'm hoping and planning for the 80-year-old me to be sitting on that verandah laughing her head off!)*

## ✏️ Activity

Think of times when, with hindsight, you've over-reacted or made a decision that didn't feel well thought out. Write them down – do they pass the verandah test?

This is a great time for you to also brainstorm what you do want to be able to say when you are sitting on the verandah.

_____

_____

_____

_____

_____

_____

# Baby steps, big jumps

**Faith is a willingness to take the next step, to see the unknown as an adventure, to launch a journey.**
**Sharon Salzberg, Buddhist Leader**

There are times in life when we just need to put one foot in front of the other and get through the day, and there are other times when we feel energetic, inspired, motivated and brave.

It's OK to cruise sometimes.

When life is hard, just do what you can to keep going. But don't miss the moments (opportunities) when everything is aligned enough for you take the first step in a different direction or, even better, a big jump.

Every once in a while you will have all that you need to take the risk, back yourself and do it. At that time, my advice is:

## " **Jump high and keep your eyes open!**"

Isn't it wonderful when you find yourself in a phase when life just works, things go your way, actions you've taken pay off, you've stretched yourself and life is good? It's often called 'being in flow'.

Chase that.

Enjoy that and bask in the glory of your baby steps and big jumps!

One thing we know for sure is that nothing in life stays the same.

Our life is like our heart line, zigzagging up and down. In order to have great things in your life, you need movement; you don't want it to go flat and straight! (I mean straight on the heart monitor, not straight as in... anyway, you get my drift.)

The bad times and bumpy bits pass but so do the good times. Most of us get a bit of everything.

Here's the thing; being a coach has shown me over and over that if we just meander along, life may well be OK, possibly even 'good'. It will be comfortable in its routines and sameness, and there will be a lack of drama, challenge and risk.

BUT, it's the big jumps that bring the biggest rewards (and excitement and sometimes drama!), the best life adventures, and the greatest learning!

 **Activity**

You're reading this book, so you must be ready (or almost). Go on, I urge you – **JUMP!** What action will you take today and tomorrow?

Consider what is required for your big jumps and if this is the right time.

_____

_____

_____

_____

_____

_____

# Strategy #13
# Solution-focused thinking

**When you focus on possibilities, you create opportunities.**

If there is only one strategy you implement, this needs to be it.

Some people find only problems, and some go beyond the problems to create solutions.

Those who consistently take the optimistic view, look for the way forward, get past the barriers and overcome the problems will mostly succeed.

Don't get me wrong, there are certainly challenges that come up for people that need and deserve attention and time. Give yourself the time and the space for reflecting on these and processing them, and to find perspective and some reality around these situations.

Sometimes you need to 'sit' in the problem a little while, talk it over with others and even vent to a trusted someone – swear a bit, have a cry or a glass of wine, or go for a run.

The problem may need some time to percolate to see what plays out, for not everything is in our control. BUT the reality is that if we don't take responsibility for finding a solution to our problem, we stay in the problem – venting, drinking, swearing, simmering – stuck!

This is about more than attitude and optimism. Being solution-focused means you will invest the time, take responsibility for what needs to happen and take action.

Are you the victim, or the person who takes the situation and reframes it? Remember, life is full of problems. Stick to your plan and be the person who adapts, finds solutions and keeps on moving.

## ✎ Activity

Reflect here on the current strategies you use when things feel hard or go wrong. When you are under pressure, what is your natural mindset? Write down and define what solution-focused thinking would look like for you. Solution-focused people are far more likely to succeed because they find a way. Keep writing!

_____

_____

_____

_____

_____

_____

_____

_____

_____

_____

_____

## Strategy #14
# Play

**Logic will get you from A to B. Imagination will take you everywhere.**
**Albert Einstein**

Please do not deny or lose your inner child! Play is a way of practising, researching, discovering and testing out new ideas and strategies. You don't have to run out to your local playground. Playfulness can be a mindset.

Young children show many wonderful traits that adults gradually lose sight of:

- they are prepared to take risks and laugh at themselves when they fail;
- they are open and honest and sincere in what they say;
- they live in the moment;
- they're interested in everything and ask millions of questions;
- their natural state is happy and cheerful;
- they talk to strangers;
- they recover from setbacks quickly;
- they spread warmth with hugs and kisses;
- they don't overthink things;
- they're energetic and enthusiastic;
- they imagine and invent;

- they love freely and generously;
- they forgive quickly;
- they soak up new learning like a sponge;
- they don't carry around baggage;
- they don't beat themselves up over bad decisions or actions;
- they mostly learn through play;
- they go after what they want; and
- they believe they can.

OK, I'm rambling a little, but I'm standing up as an advocate for adult play, using the word 'play' in a broad sense. I've always been inspired by how playful successful people can be.

Adult play (that sounds a bit weird, maybe don't say that out loud) doesn't have to involve playdough or catching bugs, although I reckon that's good fun. Adult play may be doing childlike things – paddling, playing sport, playing with pets, telling jokes, painting a picture, singing loudly, digging in dirt and so on.

Or play may be part of an attitude you adopt: how you approach a person or solve a situation or communicate a directive. Asking questions with an open mind, showing enthusiasm for a change and interacting with an appropriate sense of 'lightness' or humour are all demonstrations of 'play'.

Please make time to play and spread good cheer and watch what happens! It's the old cliché: smile and the world smiles with you. I promise you, laughter is therapeutic – it's really good for you.

##  Activity

Whatever you are doing in your work or personal life, it will go far better if you lighten things up, and if you are creative and give yourself permission to not have all the answers. Don't take yourself too seriously. Just play! (But keep it appropriate to the situation.) How can you bring more light and playfulness into your day?

What will you attract into your life if you are more playful? Consider your energy, humour and attitude here in your notes.

_____

_____

_____

_____

_____

_____

_____

_____

_____

_____

# Strategy #15
# The reality check!

**You are what you do, not what you say you will do.**
Unknown

This is where you stop and check you are telling yourself the truth about your current life. Only you know the reality of your relationships, feelings and beliefs. It is in your private and quiet moments that you are most likely to reflect on how you really feel about what you have achieved and how happy you are.

What we have already established is that quiet moments can be rare for many of us. Over time, we can a build a story that tricks us into believing that this is as good as it gets. This reality check creates some space to think more strategically and holistically about your whole life, not just parts of it. If you could step out and look from afar, what would you see?

In writing this book, I've asked people to share with me the thoughts that come to mind when I ask them to describe the reality of their current life. You will see there are both positive and negative reactions. These might get your thinking started.

My reality is:

► Opportunities will not come knocking on my door. What am I waiting for?

► I will not attract great people into my life by being mediocre. I know I am capable of more.

- I think I got tired and have forgotten to prioritise me.
- I wish I was a better friend, parent and/or leader.
- I am not sure I really know what makes me happy anymore.
- I wish I had trusted myself more.
- I am actually really proud of myself.
- I am excited to see what I do over the next five years.
- I never knew it could be this good.
- I've worked really hard for everything I have and I am happy.

Knowing, thinking and planning isn't enough – you must do. Excuses are not serving you. Blaming someone else is not a good thing. Complaining is a drag. Adapt to encompass inevitable change. Celebrate what is going really well. Acknowledge people who matter. Owning the reality of your life is an important step in writing your next chapter.

Proactivity gets you further and faster than reactivity. You must 'do great' to be great. Expecting other people to do the work for you probably won't go well. You need to find out what you don't know – but you already have what you need to succeed, so no excuses. If your reality check shows up that in your life you have everything you need and want, you can move on! This is the point in the book where you sit on your own and take a helicopter view.

Staying in your comfort zone might be pleasant, but that's all. Motivation fades – you must persevere. If you don't play, you'll never tap into your creativity.

Just stop whatever you know you should. You need to know who you are, and you need to understand and feel for others. Be good, be kind, be grateful, be courageous. You are not your job.

When reviewing your life, be humble in your success and own your mistakes. To be successful, you need to stand tall – even better, stand out.

Good communication and relationships are the keys to everything. You need to look after yourself to be your best self. The END.

### ✏️ Activity

Well, not quite the end... What's your final note to self? What does your reality check look like? What have you learnt about yourself and what is and isn't working?

Finish this sentence.

*The reality of my life is...* _____

_____

_____

_____

_____

_____

_____

_____

# Part IV
## 10 life must-haves

## If nothing is certain, anything is possible...

I need these 10 things in my life. I call them my life's must-haves (LMHs):

1. Sandy feet
2. Adventure
3. Messy moments
4. Kindness
5. Stillness
6. A grateful heart
7. Patting dogs
8. Hugging
9. Stealing
10. Escape.

Maybe one or two will resonate with you. Or perhaps you have a long list of your own that you will be inspired to write out and live by every day (there's space for that at the end of this section). In your next chapter, you will be evolving and growing. This makes looking after yourself so important. Remember busy is not sexy. Having some go-to strategies is critical to your wellbeing. These are my non-negotiables when it comes to what I know I need to be the best version of me.

**LMH #1**

# Sandy feet

Where is the place you can visit that feeds you emotionally, physically and spiritually? The beach is my place. But there are also so many other perfect small moments I can notice or include in my day, even when I can't get to the beach. I can take a little time to meditate and imagine myself at the beach with sandy feet.

There is research to support this imagining skill – it's called visualisation and it is very powerful. I close my eyes and I can smell the salt air, see the children playing and feel the sand between my toes, and it refuels me. What's magic about this is that just 10 minutes of imagining can totally shift my energy.

What will your sandy feet moments look like in your next chapter?

 **Do not underestimate the power of the ocean, the joy of giving and how it feels to breathe."**

## LMH #2
# Adventure

The human spirit needs comfort. It also needs newness. Adventure can be found at home, at work, in the community, on a holiday, anywhere! This is about those moments that make your heart beat faster. It's the thrill of not knowing, it's the fun of embarrassing yourself, it's the challenge of doing something different, it's the joy in achievement. In my world, travel, motherhood and mistakes are where some of my greatest learning has come from.

New experiences show us things about ourselves and the world we live in. It can be as simple as getting in the car and just driving with no plan or destination. Or as big as climbing a mountain. Adventure is good for you!

If you were planning a new adventure, where would you go? What would you do?

## LMH #3
# Messy moments

There are days when you should let everything go, whatever your version of that is. Not every day can you (nor should you) be a high-performer, full of awesomeness. Some days you just need to say f**k you universe, I am staying in my PJs and eating cereal from the box while I watch TV.

There are moments when we need to cry, be vulnerable and feel sorry for ourselves. Life is messy sometimes, and we are allowed to be messy in it, for a while.

This book is not about being 'perfect'. You are a unique and complex being and you will mess up sometimes – make mistakes, feel loss, get hurt and generally have some dumbass moments. Of course, the emotionally-responsible-high-performing you will pull it together soon. Right?

Do you have a strategy for looking after the messy you?

**P.S.** I admire messy people who don't always get it right but who, in their messiness, hold onto their integrity and are fiercely loyal to the people they love.

## LMH #4
# Kindness

The world would be different if everyone made kindness a non-negotiable. It's sometimes better to be kind than to be right. You've probably heard that before, but I want to say it here because kindness matters so much in this harsh world. And kindness is good for you. How often have you been kind and regretted it? My assumption would be rarely.

Kindness is great for your health, it changes your world and it nearly always finds its way back to you. There is something quite practical about practising kindness too. My experience in working with leaders and organisations across the world clearly indicates that we associate kindness with integrity, generosity, respect and compassion. And guess what? Kind people are the people we most trust. Being generous with your time and kindness towards others is super attractive to most people.

How can you be consciously kind every day?

> *What you do makes a difference, and you have to decide what kind of difference you want to make.*
> **Jane Goodall**

**LMH #5**

# Stillness

The body and the mind both need physical activity to be healthy. However, it is just as important, if not more so, to give yourself stillness. It's when your body heals, your head processes and your heart feels. We live in a fast-paced and ever-changing world. What do we miss when we don't have dedicated time every day to be in stillness? Stillness is directly linked to good health.

It is a fact that people who meditate lower their blood pressure and heart rate, for example. Stillness can be as simple as closing your eyes in the car before your next meeting. (Not while you're driving, obviously.) Breathe and just be still for a few minutes or an hour. Find a way!

What would be different for you if stillness were part of your everyday life?

# A grateful heart

There are gratitude books and journals everywhere you look so, just for fun, I've included here some of the inserts from my personal records from the last few weeks as I wrote this book.

- I would like to thank my bed. I miss you so much when I am away. Even though we are often separated, you are always in my thoughts.

- I want to thank nature for the sound of the ocean and sand between my toes. For thunderstorms at night and for peonies (the most beautiful flowers ever to exist). But if you could get rid of flies that would be amazing. I am not grateful for flies even though I understand they are an important part of the food chain.

- Thank you, spaghetti bolognaise. I really appreciate that you are always better the next day. You have never let me down.

- Thank you to all the old couples who hold hands on the beach. I love you so much for doing that.

- A big thank you to Italy. Yep. The entire country. You feel like home. You make me sleep and slow down. You make carbs OK and your buildings speak to me. I will come back soon I promise.

- Thank you to all the women who showed me the way. There are so many of you.

- Thank you to the men who allow me to stay optimistic about love and to all the men who backed me to be whoever I wanted to be.

- I want to acknowledge the people who hold open lift doors when I'm running to get there. That's such a great thing to do. Bless your cotton socks.

- To the person who invented massage. You are a legend. I had one today and it was the purest form of indulgence I can imagine.

- Thank you to Ben Stiller. You make me laugh. I just watched *Walter Mitty* for the 1,489th time.

- Musicians!!! I can't imagine not having music that moves me. I am so grateful that music is a thing. It's a connecter across all humankind.

- I'd like to thank Albert Einstein today. I reckon you were a top bloke and I wish we could have had dinner. Can we meet up in the next life?

- A huge thank you to toothbrushes and whoever invented them. I'm pretty sure kissing wouldn't be a thing if we didn't have you. And kissing is great.

---

**grati|tude** – *noun*

the quality of being thankful; readiness to show appreciation for and to return kindness.

---

 **Gratitude does change you.**"

163

What are you grateful for? Yes, you! There's much hype around the art of being grateful and, in my view, this is not a passing fad. The benefits of feeling and recognising what you are grateful for are awesome. Gratitude brings perspective, allows us to say thank you and recognises what is bringing happiness and learning to our life. Make this a daily habit. Start by making a list right here of what you are feeling grateful for today!

*I am grateful for...*

_____

_____

_____

_____

_____

_____

_____

_____

_____

_____

# Patting dogs

Since my daughter Mabel was little, she hasn't been able to walk past a dog without stopping to pat it. I commented recently that she's always so happy when she sees a dog. Her reply to me was, 'People are so interesting, mum; it's amazing what they tell me.' Um... 'What?' I didn't quite understand her point because she is smarter than I am.

She explained that when you are nice and friendly to someone's dog, they smile at you and will often tell you something important to them. Her most recent example was the elderly lady who asked Mabel how old she was and shared that she was missing her granddaughter a lot. So they talked for a little while about the lady's granddaughter, where she lived and why. Mabel asked when they would see each other again. (Bless her cotton socks.)

We need to find ways to connect with our community. It's important that we feel we are part of something that is bigger than us. There's a chemical reaction that happens when we feel a sense of belonging. Having strategies in place that allow you to be in the moment with someone else is one of life's greatest gifts. Stop and pat a dog!

What's your version of patting dogs? Be specific and find a way.

## LMH #8
# Hugging

OK, I know there are two types of people – huggers and non-huggers. I am such a hugger that I can take personal offence if you don't want to hug me back. Hugging is my love language. It's part of my 'brand'. It's what I do.

I do attempt to hug with respect (not really). I hug people I love and people I've never met before. I understand that we need to be cautious and respectful in the current environment, especially at work! I know plenty of men who feel it's inappropriate to hug their female colleagues. But if we can just keep things simple for a moment, let me share why I think hugging is one of life's must-haves.

Hugging communicates so much about what we are feeling. It can be comforting or simply about the joy of seeing someone. Hugging can say I'm sorry, I love you, I'm so happy to meet you and are you OK? Hugging releases oxytocin from the brain to make you feel good, which is the most natural mood elevator you can have in your life. There are all kinds of research that shows us that hugging reduces stress and actually slows down our heart rate.

For all non-huggers reading this, I do understand. If you don't hug, find a different way to create this experience for you and others. In a crazy busy world, hugging is one of the few things we do with another human that doesn't cost us a thing and is really good for us. No devices allowed! Hugging is the purist and most beautiful form of communication.

*I have learned that there is more power in a good hug than in a thousand meaningful words.*

**Ann Hood**

## LMH #9
# Stealing

Now, don't go and do anything illegal; stealing is a very dramatic word, but it got your attention!

What I'm suggesting here is that the world is amazing and it's full of amazing people, so perhaps there are some things you could 'borrow' from them.

So often I see people inspired by something they have seen in someone else, and then the moment passes without acting upon that inspiration. They get busy again and what went before is now forgotten. So that I don't forget those incredible moments, every day I consciously look for what I can learn from others. Every single day I get ideas and new thinking from the people around me and from my environment. And I write them down, I meditate on them and I share what I've learnt with others.

Imitation is a form of flattery. Some of the greatest writers, CEOs, designers and teachers on this planet do what they do so that others can grow and take what they've created and translate it into something meaningful in their life.

Of course, we should credit people and celebrate them, but take what resonates and add it to your own plan in this book. Look at the leaders in the world and the language they use. Reflect on conversations you've had with people you respect and identify what strategies they used to gain your respect. Pick up all those awesome books you've read and find one thing that could make a difference to how you're living your life.

Before your start the next chapter in you, do an audit on the life moments and people who have made your heart beat faster. What can you take and make your own?

*We have always been shameless about stealing great ideas.*

**Steve Jobs**

**Find a way to capture your moments of inspiration. Carry a journal, make a collage or write a book!**

## LMH #10
# Escape

There are moments, hours and/or days when you should ignore everyone and everything. I believe it's absolutely part of the human condition to need to turn everything off sometimes.

I'm not talking about making time for meditation or beach-walking, because those activities require intention and a plan to do them. What I mean by escaping is time to literally have no plan, no responsibilities and total freedom to do whatever it is you feel like in the moment.

There are so many ways we can escape the reality of life for a bit. Travel does that for me and so does a great movie. Some people sleep to escape, and others listen to music. For all the parents out there, just reading this is making you laugh, I know! (Time for yourself, what's that?)

My experience as a coach tells me that we are all scheduling our lives to the minute. We plan everything from date night to exercise. Part of your plan should be having moments where there is no plan. Sometimes when I suggest this to clients they feel it is too indulgent. But I ask you, what are the consequences of *not* having time and space to rest your head and heart?

e|leuthero|mania – *noun*

an intense and irresistible desire for freedom.

## Activity

Using my list as inspiration, take a few moments now to consider what your life must-haves are. These are critical to your wellbeing, so write them down and think about how you can incorporate them into your day, your week and your year.

_____

_____

_____

_____

_____

_____

_____

_____

_____

_____

_____

_____

_____

_____

**This escapism is not a nice-to-have, it's a life must-have!**

# Part V
## Your story's next chapter

As a result of the challenges you've faced, the reflections you've made after reading this book and the decisions you're starting to make about what you *reaaaally* want, you're now ready to take action.

My guidelines are these. When you're ready to turn your notes into your story, it should be no more than six pages in length, and it should take no more than 10 minutes to read out and be listened to. This will give you a structure and force you to really think about what matters most to you about the journey you are on. If you only have 10 minutes to tell people about you, what do you most want them to know, feel and understand?

Take a holistic approach – think about your personal *and* working life. You may need to get a little creative to stay within the 'I am' format – for example, for the first statement, *'I am from a little town called Gympie, the eldest daughter of...'*. Talk about yourself honestly but in positive terms – be kind to you, and proud of you and what you have achieved so far.

The following sections are prompts for reflection. (Your final statement won't be a series of 'I am...' sentences.)

Let's get into it.

# How are you, really?

How many times a day are you greeted with those three little words 'How are you?' I bet you couldn't count. We all know it's usually a question that only demands a simple 'Good, thanks'. But have you ever noticed how people get uncomfortable when you give them something else – like an honest answer to this question, particularly if you're having a crap day?

So, I'm asking you now, *'How are you?' 'How are you really?'*

It's time to gain some deeper insight into how you currently feel about the various areas of your life. Many years of working as a coach have shown me that the items in the activity below are the big-ticket ones when it comes to creating an emotionally healthy life.

You might be feeling that your career is booming, but at the cost of a significant relationship. Or perhaps your financial situation is strong, but at the cost of your health. It's a challenge to get all areas of your life working in harmony, but this activity will support your thinking in where you need to make compromises, do more or stop.

### ✐ Activity

Tick the two or three areas you need or want to devote more time or effort to in order to create the life you want, rather than the one you may be living as a default.

☐ Relationships      ☐ Career
☐ Home environment      ☐ Fun
☐ Health      ☐ Finances
☐ Learning opportunities      ☐ Adventure

To help you work this out, consider these questions:

- Are my priorities right?
- Am I living in alignment with my values? (Refer to your previous notes.)
- Am I investing my time and energy where it will most affect whatever success means for me?
- How do I feel when I reflect on the seven main areas of my life?
- What is working really well for me?
- What feedback would others give me on the choices I am making and how I spend my time?
- Is there something I have been ignoring in my life that now needs to be structured into my plan?

## What are your strengths?

This section is primarily about identifying the strengths you have that will support your success. However, it also encompasses thinking about the competencies you aspire to have and that you believe are necessary for greater success. Earlier in this book I said that your uniqueness is your greatest asset. When you can identify what makes you an original and what your signature strengths are you can tell others!

'Success' should be seen as success in a holistic sense – that is, in your whole life rather than just at work. What are your strengths emotionally, intellectually, physically, socially and environmentally?

 **Activity**

What would be in your top five list of attributes that contribute to a successful life *and* work? Tick any of those in the following list that particularly resonate with you – and even integrate them into your 'I am...' statement.

- [ ] Managing ambiguity and adapting
- [ ] Forgiveness
- [ ] Generous with time, knowledge and kindness
- [ ] Consistent honesty and authenticity
- [ ] The trusted adviser
- [ ] Intelligence (IQ)
- [ ] A high-impact communicator
- [ ] The perfect blend of information and inspiration
- [ ] Brings clarity and harmony to the room
- [ ] An ability to collaborate and/or innovate
- [ ] Leadership that demonstrates positive/optimistic attitude, courage, perseverance and boldness
- [ ] Integrity in all aspects of life
- [ ] An ability to unlearn and then learn again
- [ ] Emotional and physical fitness
- [ ] Brings fun wherever possible
- [ ] Embraces uniqueness and doesn't have to know the answers
- [ ] Curious about everything
- [ ] Sets high goals and holds self accountable
- [ ] Relationship builder (in work and personal life), risk-taker, leader, collaborative, tenacious
- [ ] Empowering of self and others.

Think about what success will look like in five years as you look back on this time in your life. If you are living your best life and being the best version of you, what inherent strengths support that already, and what do you need further?

The list I have created above reflects some of the strengths I have consistently observed in my successful clients; however, your list may be quite different. These serve only to prompt your thinking – your strengths are uniquely yours.

# Building momentum

As you begin the process of change, it's important to gain momentum. No doubt there will be days when your motivation is low – it happens to the best of us – but, ideally, you will find some flow with this work and remember what your commitments are. I have developed a couple of strategies to help keep you focused.

**Learn how to learn more about yourself.** Continue to increase your self-insight by finding opportunities to observe yourself and to draw out the implications of what you observe. Get into the habit of analysing your responses to new experiences and asking for feedback. This should be a habit!

**Assess your current job.** How well does your current job fulfil your career needs? Does it use your talents, meet your needs and fulfil your values? We know that careers play a big part in how we feel about life.

**Plan ahead.** Does your life need a redesign to be more fulfilling in the future? Or perhaps you are really happy with where you are and what you have achieved, but know you will want more.

As you contemplate future life decisions, are you doing what's required now to set you up for success? Do you need additional education or training? Do you favour certain kinds of lateral or geographical moves?

**Communicate your needs.** Who needs to know the plans you are making for yourself? The world is full of amazing, talented and wise people. Let them know you are here and tap into their knowledge. Are there people in your organisation with whom you should share some of your plans so that they can advocate for you? Do you and members of your family need to discuss your goals to make a better overall life plan?

**Become active in managing your own life.** It's no one else's job to do this for you. If you don't proactively get up most days and check in with yourself, all of a sudden you will wake up one day and be five years older. You are the CEO of your life. What do you need to do right now?

## What not to do!

Adults are very good at under- and/or overthinking (depending on our nature). We're good at looking for the quick and easy option. We are sensitive to others' criticism, we self-sabotage and we procrastinate. So don't beat yourself up; rather, push through these 'normal' behaviours.

Here is a list of stumbling blocks I see over and over again, and my suggestions on how to avoid them. I'm a coach so I prefer positive language; however, I need to get your attention here!

- ☒ **DON'T...** expect everyone to be happy about your newfound self-focus, attitudes, beliefs, behaviours and success. There are probably lots of people in your life who like you just the way you are, and making changes is uncomfortable for them. Be prepared to lose some people along the way.

- ☒ **DON'T...** focus on everything you failed at, don't like about yourself or need to do better. If your plan going forward is about all your gaps and flaws, you will just end up having well developed weaknesses. Spend time on what you are passionate about, because you're probably good at that.

☒ **DON'T...** wait. The opportunities might not come to you. Money won't suddenly appear in your bank account. Tomorrow never comes. Monday is just a day of the week. You won't magically have more information or education or motivation tomorrow. If you want awesome, be awesome and do what others won't. And start doing it now!

☒ **DON'T...** expect anything to change if you don't. You can't trick the universe. There's no easy way out. There's no magic or secret fix. It's not enough to read or plan or buy or talk. You must do! Real change will require consistent effort from you every day.

☒ **DON'T...** be unrealistic and set yourself up to fail before you start. You will likely have bad or sad days, and falter or fail sometimes. This book is not about rampant (unachievable) positivity. It's about making conscious choices, showing resilience, persevering, being present in each day and allowing for your 'humanness'. Be kind to you.

☒ **DON'T...** make your past the story of your future. People often get 'stuck' in who and how they've been before.

☒ **DON'T...** lose yourself. This is not about erasing the core of who you are. Rather, this is about adopting and adapting some new behaviours – the behaviours of successful people. The amazing thing about you is that you are uniquely you. There is no other individual on this planet who has the same story as you.

Own your past, know your values and listen to your instincts. Be authentic and true to you. Create a future that is about you and for you.

# Writing the next chapter

**Life isn't about finding yourself; it's about creating yourself.**

**George Bernard Shaw**

The following are prompts to encourage you to think more broadly and deeply about who you are, what your life's journey has been so far, and where you want to 'go' in the future. You could choose from any or all of these statements to formulate your story – or add any others that feel more relevant.

### ✎ Activity

Finish these sentences:

*I am* (life influences – for example, family, social, cultural, economic, experiential)

_____

_____

_____

_____

*I am* currently (life circumstances – for example, family, social, cultural, economic, experiential)

_____

_____

_____

_____

*I am* in my personal life (role taken, reputation as, known for, passionate about)

_____

_____

_____

*I am* very aware that (most powerful life moment)

_____

_____

_____

*I am* in my work (role usually taken in team)

_____

_____

_____

*I am* committed to (values, people, goals)

_____

_____

_____

*I am* letting go (experiences that don't define who I am now)

_____

_____

_____

*I am* grateful for (learning lessons, gifts, moments)

_____

_____

_____

*I am* (current priorities)

_____

_____

_____

*I am* (strengths)

_____

_____

_____

*I am* most proud of

_____

_____

_____

*I am* someone who gets really (excited, sad or angry about)

_____

_____

_____

**I *am*** (challenges, weaknesses)

_____

_____

_____

**I *am*** (goals, vision, ideal, dream, wishes)

_____

_____

_____

**I *am*** (hobbies, sport and so on)

_____

_____

_____

**I *am*** (issue, relationship or circumstance in your life that you would like to better understand or change, over the course of time)

_____

_____

_____

**I *am*** working on (goals, self-improvement)

_____

_____

_____

*I am* (according to my friends)

_____

_____

_____

*I am* (trusting that my next chapter will bring)

_____

_____

_____

*I am* (according to work colleagues)

_____

_____

_____

*I am* (according to me)

_____

_____

_____

Having answered all these questions as honestly and fully as possible, you are going to be a giant leap closer to answering the ultimate existential question: **Who am I?**

This is really the most important question there is. For with the knowledge that comes from answering this question, you can make informed choices and decisions about the next chapter in your story.

In essence, what you are uncovering is this:

- **The private you:** your fears, dreams, secrets, insecurities and hidden and untapped potential.

- **The inner you:** your values, beliefs, thinking, personality, habits, experiences and knowledge.

- **The public you:** what others see, know, expect of you and feel about you.

- **The external you:** the way you look, present yourself, interact, behave, decide, respond, react and affect others. Your voice, your beliefs, your heart, your mind, your vision, your strengths and your story.

You are the only person who knows how you feel and what you think in any moment. You are a unique human with an inner rockstar (potential) waiting to be let loose. Find yourself and be that!

In the corporate world, we talk about a 'unique positioning statement'. (You might understand it as your 'elevator pitch'.) Professionals refine and practise this, so they can strategically talk about where they've been, what they've achieved, what they're about and what they have to offer. And they do it succinctly.

What would you tell me about you if you only had 45 seconds? What would you say in an interview if you were asked to talk about yourself?

Know yourself and know how to tell people about you, authentically, yet with your best foot forward (figuratively, not meaning wear your best shoes).

Practise in front of a mirror with loved ones and with your truth tellers. Whether you're a mum at home, a uni student or a budding entrepreneur, watch for what is different when you know who you are and what you have to offer – in the world, in relationships, in your career and in ambition.

Think well of you. Focus on your strengths. Believe that you can take action to cross that gap between where you are now and where you want to be.

Learn, love, achieve… whatever rocks your boat, sets your heart singing, and makes for a life well lived.

### Activity

Write your 'I am…' statement here.

*I am* _____

_____

_____

_____

_____

_____

*I cannot teach you anything;*
*I can only make you stop and think.*

**Commonly attributed to Socrates**

# Look after you

So we are nearly at the end of this ride together. I couldn't finish this book without telling you that I want you to look after you.

We all know the old analogy of putting your own oxygen mask on first. There are times when you need to be kind, patient and nurturing with yourself. One of the themes in coaching successful people is that they are their own worst self-critic. They are highly competent in identifying what they need to do better or where they messed up. It takes up headspace and really is not helpful.

Here are my tips on how to ensure you are paying attention to the good stuff you need to move forward.

1. If it feels wrong, it probably is

2. Let go of what is not in your control

3. Stay away from the energy vampires

4. Trust you because your instincts rarely let you down

5. Laugh often and make others laugh too

6. Be careful what story you're telling yourself about you

7. Don't give up on the possibility of having it all

8. Eat soup because I said so

9. Sleep and then sleep some more

10. Mindless TV really is OK sometimes

11. Know you are loved

12. There is someone out there who wishes they had your life

13. Do what you can manage on your bad days

14. It's possible that life will be better than you planned

15. Don't compare yourself to others

16. Every moment in the story of you has its place

17. You will be OK; in fact, you will be more than OK

18. Move your body as if you like yourself

19. Like all things this too shall pass

20. We are all in this together, doing the best we can.

## Activity

Make notes here on a good day, so that you can come back to this page on a bad day. Write down the words here that will describe how you feel on your very best days – words like inspired, safe, rested, on purpose, loved, successful, light, happy, valued, excited, challenged and nurtured...

_____

_____

_____

_____

_____

_____

_____

_____

_____

_____

# A final few words from me

Thank you for reading this book. I really appreciate your trust and time. I am very passionate about learning and sharing, so this book was a natural next step for me. It was a fun, challenging and rewarding process to collate all my learnings and thinking right here for you.

My hope is that this book will serve you for many years to come. Please keep it safe and value the work you have done. You have lots of chapters to write, plan and live yet. The questions in this book will remain relevant as you review and reflect on the life you are living, so please come back and read this book again when the time is right.

Congratulations in advance! Sometimes timing is everything. Things click into place and you own your own stuff. You recognise how far you have come and feel grateful for the lessons that went before.

May this book have come into your possession at just the right time. Your life will be many things, but mostly I trust you will do the work required to create whatever success means for you. I want you to feel proud of the person you have become and fought hard to be.

Unfortunately, there will be a few who read this and won't do what's required. That's inevitable. Just know that this book will be waiting for you down the track.

If you do write and consciously create your next chapter, I am so happy for you. May your future be everything you need and want. I truly believe that life is meant to have moments of magic. We all have an inner warrior ready to fight for things that matter. What I want for all of us is to live a life that is not as expected!

So I share this final quote with you, which means a lot to me; it is a reflection of how I live my life. I wish I had been clever enough to write it myself.

*She had a gypsy soul and a warrior spirit.*
*She made no apologies for her wild heart.*
*She left normal and regular to explore the*
*outskirts of magical and extraordinary.*

**Michelle Rose Gilman**

Take care of you.

Lots of love from me to you, your family and friends.

See you again soon.

*Lisa xxx*

# A message from Stacey

## Hi everyone

I am Lisa's Executive Manager here at The Coach Place. I know! It's a big job but someone has to do it.

If you are vaguely interested in having Lisa speak at your next event or doing some work with your team, please email me: stacey@thecoachplace.com.

This same email address can cope with your influx of coaching inquiries and feedback on this book. Lisa and our team would love to hear what you think.

So who asks Lisa to speak to their people and who may benefit? Everyone! Anyone! She speaks at huge events and small, to new graduates through to those already at the top of their game, to those struggling and others who are thriving. Lisa is just as comfortable speaking with a group of 12 senior leaders as she is speaking to a room of 1,000 people.

We look forward to hearing from you and trust you love the book.

- Instagram – thecoachplace
- Facebook – coachplaceglobal
- LinkedIn – search Lisa Stephenson
- YouTube – search Lisa Stephenson

Or visit us at:

- www.readmefirst.com.au for more information about the book
- www.thecoachplace.com for more information on our programs and talented team of coaches

Like Lisa, I am a natural hugger, so please pretend there is a hug attached to this page.

Stace

# Thank you

I am grateful for these people in my life.

To my children, James, William and Mabel. There were days when I didn't know how we would do it on our own. Turns out we are the Stephenson tribe. We are tight, connected and I am so proud to be your mum. I know there's stuff we miss. I know sometimes you eat cereal for dinner. But I promised you education, good teeth and a home full of love, and I hope that's what I'm delivering. Thank you for encouraging me to write this book and for always telling me everything is OK. Mabel, I want to be like you when I grow up. William, I love you so much my heart hurts. James, you are extraordinary and I just can't wait to see what you do in the world.

I literally couldn't have done any of this without my parents, who are generous with love and time beyond all measure. Mum, you stopped everything to support me in raising my three children when it felt as if the world was ending, and you've been in every part of this business since we started at my kitchen bench. You really are Super Nana. Dad, what would the world be like if every girl had a dad who loved like you? Thank you for showing my children what a good man is. Marc, you really are the favourite and I don't know how I got so lucky to have you as a brother. To have a sister-in-law like you, Michelle, is a blessing.

Anna Meirelles, Kathy Rodwell, Chris Hughes and Catherine Moynihan for truly making the Coach Place Global team everything that it is known for. You've been in this with me from the beginning. You always do more than is required. I am so proud of every single event and coaching session you have delivered. Lives have changed because of the work you do. And to 'my' Stacey Henschell for being my person. You are at the core of everything we do, you tell me the truth and I trust you more than words. To all the other incredible coaches, facilitators and contractors who shared the journey at some point and contributed to our purpose, thank you.

Mr Craig Harper, it's eight years since we met and you are one of the greatest gifts the universe has delivered me. You are unconditional, generous and oh so wise. I've learnt to ignore the swearing and treasure the laughter. Thank you for your support, time, guidance and belief in me. Do yourself a favour everyone and check out www.craigharper.net.

Aneka Manners, you are smart, intuitive, creative, entrepreneurial and the bestest friend I could ask for (and you always have wine). You are an inspiration to me. Please go to www.anekamanners.com.au to see the designs that will dominate the world one day.

David Hornery was the man who trusted me with his people when I didn't know I could do what I now do. He remains my mentor and, more importantly, someone I love to hang out with.

Charmaine Waugh, because you were invoice 000000001. The very first client who said yes and told me others would too. Jacqui Gross, you have been there for all of it – first bra and blue light discos included. Childhood friends who ended up following each other all around the world. I love you.

Cindy Batchelor, the hugest thank you for being my advocate, friend and the leader who shows us the way. Megan Collins for being the client who became a treasured friend and taught me what it means to be amazeballs. Melanie Hilton for trusting me with the things that matter to you. Natalie Thomas for making work the most fun it could be. Jon Eddy for laughing at my jokes and expecting me to laugh at yours. Andrew O'Brien because you never do as you're told and you do it with heart.

To Kim Anderson, who is the hair and make-up fairy who became a friend. Nehemiah Richardson for telling anyone who will listen that I'm awesome. Alastair McGibbon and Tim Dinning for working on planet Lisa with your cameras and talent. Kate Colley, you are a gem for making that very first call and partnering with me to make it thrive. To Maria and the team at Via Boffe Café for letting me write this book at the quiet table in the corner for hours on end. To Leanne Hegarty, Debsta Firth and Colin and Lesley Moore for being the Nokia crew who became long-serving laughing buddies and precious friends. Karen Telfer, because you are the friend every girl needs and Carol Campbell for being everything that you are.

My uni crew who bring music festivals, inappropriate games and make me feel like I am still 17 – Christine Pritchard, Tim Reddan, Nathan Lange, Brendan and Helen McKenzie, and Sarah Reddan because you married Tim and we love you for it.

Thank you to Barbra (Brabra) Nicholson for telling me in the early days, and forever after, that I can do it. To my friend Sue who showed me that single mums rock. Tommy Jackett, you are a talented film-maker and so much fun to work with. To my ex-husband who gave me the lessons that shaped me, the resilience that challenged me and the three beautiful babies I wanted and can't imagine not having. Full love and respect to each of the legends who provided testimonials for this book.

To my publisher, Lesley, who has held my hand all the way while promising champagne when we become a bestseller. You said yes to an unpublished want-to-be author when others didn't. Jo Johnson, the Content Coach, you taught me the skill of writing a book and told me not to panic. Your patience and advice was never-ending.

I have such a huge family that I can't list them all here. To my aunties, uncles, cousins, Ann and my 93-year-old grandad, huge love to you all.

There are clearly lots of beautiful people in my life. Lots. And there's no way to list them all here. Confidentiality contracts are common for me, but you all know who you are and how much your trust means. To do this work is the greatest privilege I can imagine. I get to hear things that you've never said out loud to anyone and have the honour of being your mirror. I appreciate that you leave your ego at the door, come prepared and show the vulnerability that is needed to work on yourself. When you made the big jumps I cheered quietly for you and when you didn't think you could anymore, I carried the belief for you. I loved hearing the story of you, where you've been and where you want to go. It's so very awesome to be the facilitator of your thinking, dreams and thoughts. You made me laugh and cry. I learnt something from you too. Thank you to every single person who delivered their 'I am...' statement. This book exists because we all went on this journey together. Your courage sits with me always. Congratulations on being you.

The end of this book, and the
beginning of your next chapter...